Motherhood and Work in Contemporary Japan

This book explores the employment of Japanese women born in the 1960s and 1970s who experienced childbirth and raised children in the 1990s and the early 2000s. During this period, the Japanese economy experienced a severe recession. It has affected the firm-specific internal labour market and employment practices, which in turn are thought to have greatly influenced Japanese women's employment. On the other hand, the fertility rate declined and social policies to support women's employment began to be implemented after the 1990s. This book explores how these labour market structure and social policies interact to affect Japanese women's employment. The book first analyses the employment patterns of women born between the 1920s and 1970s and examines how they have varied among different birth cohorts. Then the employment behaviour of women before and after childbirth through the post-child-rearing period, as well as the working career of single mothers, is explored for women born in the 1960s and 1970s. Based on the data analyses, the concluding part of this book discusses how changes in the labour market and women's employment support policies during the 1990s and early 2000s interactively influenced employment behaviour of Japanese women, and some suggestions are put forward for changing women's employment during the child-rearing years.

Junko Nishimura is Professor at Meisei University, Tokyo.

Routledge Research on Gender in Asia Series

Motherhood and Work in Contemporary Japan

Junko Nishimura

Routledge
Taylor & Francis Group

LONDON AND NEW YORK

First published 2016 by Routledge

2 Park Square, Milton Park, Abingdon, Oxfordshire OX14 4RN
711 Third Avenue, New York, NY 10017

*Routledge is an imprint of the Taylor & Francis Group,
an informa business*

First issued in paperback 2017

British Library Cataloguing in Publication Data
A catalogue record for this book is available from the British Library

Library of Congress Cataloging-in-Publication Data
Names: Nishimura, Junko, author.
Title: Motherhood and work in contemporary Japan / Junko Nishimura.
Description: Abingdon, Oxon ; New York, NY : Routledge, 2017. | Series:
   Routledge research on gender in Asia ; 12 | Includes bibliographical
   references and index.
Identifiers: LCCN 2015046311 | ISBN 9781138943667 (hardback) |
   ISBN 9781315727943 (e-book)
Subjects: LCSH: Working mothers—Japan. | Women—Employment—
   Japan. | Married women—Employment—Japan. | Work and family—
   Japan. | Women—Japan—Social conditions.
Classification: LCC HQ759.48 .N57 2017 | DDC 305.40952—dc23
LC record available at http://lccn.loc.gov/2015046311

ISBN: 978-1-138-94366-7 (hbk)
ISBN: 978-0-8153-6876-2 (pbk)

Typeset in Times New Roman
by Apex CoVantage, LLC

To my husband and children

Contents

Figures

Tables

Acknowledgments

The data from the Japanese Panel Survey of Consumers (JPSC) is provided by the Institute for Research on Household Economics. Much of the research on which the book is based was supported by JSPS KAKENHI Grant Number 25380704 from the Japan Society for the Promotion of Science. I am thankful for the support of these institutions. Two anonymous reviewers as well as Simon Bates, the editor Routledge, provided very helpful comments on an early draft of the book. A part of the material in this book is from my published book in Japanese entitled *Kosodate to Shigoto no Shakaigaku* by Kobundo Inc. in 2014. I am grateful for the Japanese publisher for letting me have the opportunity to use the work here.

1 Introduction

The Japanese women's employment puzzle

Japanese women's employment has shown a pattern that differs in three distinct ways from the ones observed in industrial societies in other countries: (1) an overall increase in the employment rate of women has not been accompanied by an increase in the employment rate of women with young children; (2) higher educational attainment among women has not contributed to an increase in the employment rate of women with children; and (3) part-time employment is not an attractive way of working for women with young children. These three points are discussed ahead in detail.

First, in many countries, an overall increase in the employment rate of women has been accompanied by an increase in the employment rate of women with young children. In Japan, however, the employment rate of women with young children has remained low even as the overall employment rate of women has increased. According to the Labour Force Survey, the employment rate of women aged 15 to 64 increased from 54.9% in 1987 to 59.6% in 1997 and then to 61.9% in 2007. Yet, the employment rate of women in households with children under the age of 3 has remained low, with rates at 27.6% in 1987, 27.8% in 1997 and 33.2% in 2007 (calculated from published tables of the Employment Status Survey by Statistics Bureau, Ministry of Internal Affairs and Communications, Japan). This anomaly between the employment rates for the two categories of women has rarely been observed in other societies. For example, according to the Organisation for Economic Cooperation and Development (OECD, 2011), which conducted a cross-national study on the employment of women with children, the employment rate of women with children under the age of 16 years is over 80% in Sweden and 70% in Denmark; that of women with children under 2 years old is approximately 70% in both these countries. Hungary and the Czech Republic exhibit a pattern similar to that in Japan, but the phenomenon of low employment of only women with young children is quite uncommon among OECD countries.

Second, in Japan, women's higher educational attainment has not contributed to an increase in the overall employment rate of women or to that of women with children. Analysing the employment patterns of birth cohorts of the 1940s and 1950s, Brinton (1993) demonstrated that higher educational attainment did not prevent women from exiting the labour force upon marriage. Using data including the 1960s birth cohort, Yu (2009) showed that the number of years in school curbed women's resignation from their jobs upon marriage but did not affect their likelihood of resigning upon the birth of their first child.

This pattern differs from those observed in many industrialised societies. For example, Vlasblom and Schippers (2004) showed that in EU countries (West Germany, Spain, France, Italy, the Netherlands and the United Kingdom), women with higher education were more likely to be involved in the labour force than women without such education, and among women with higher education, having young children had a smaller effect on their likelihood of exiting the labour force. In addition, Brewster and Rindfuss (2000) reviewed research on EU countries, the United States, Canada and Australia and concluded that women with higher education were less likely to quit their jobs. Even when they did, they were more likely to re-enter the labour force earlier. They argued that such effects of education were robust across time and different data sets. As discussed later, although the higher education enrolment rate of Japanese women has become as high as that of Japanese men, this rate has not contributed, in turn, to an increase in the employment rate of women with young children. This phenomenon is peculiar to Japan.

Third, temporary or part-time work has not become an effective way of keeping women with young children in the labour force. The percentage of women employed part-time increases when their children enter school. While their children are very young, however, Japanese women are more likely to choose not to work instead of working part-time. This is also peculiar to Japan.

According to Sundström (1997), among women in Sweden who gave birth to their first child from 1988 to 1990, only about 2% remained outside the labour force around the time of the birth and less than 5% left their full-time positions to exit the labour force completely. Sundström argued that in Sweden, this was because women with young children could exercise their right to take childcare leave and reduce their working hours and were even guaranteed the right to return to their full-time positions. Moreover, they were also able to work part-time with social security benefits, paid vacation time and job security. In the Netherlands, the employment rate of women aged 15 to 64 years ranged from 30% to 40% in 1980 but increased to 70% in 2009. In addition, the employment rate of women with children below the age of 2 reached approximately 70% in 2005 (OECD, 2011). An increase in part-time work opportunities supported this improvement. In fact, 75% of women aged 25 to 54 years with children were working part-time in 2009 (OECD, 2012).

These findings from the related literature show that part-time labour is an attractive employment option for women soon after childbirth in some countries. However, the same cannot be said for part-time work in Japan. In the following section, the reasons for this are discussed.

Can labour supply factors explain Japan's peculiarities?

One might expect labour supply factors to explain the peculiarities of Japanese women's employment. However, this does not appear to be the case. As in other industrialised societies, several factors would be expected to increase women's employment in Japan: (1) an increase in the average age at first marriage; (2) longer life expectancy and lower fertility; (3) higher educational attainment; and (4) an increase in the divorce rate. Considering these factors, Japan should do more to push women into the labour force. Table 1.1 shows changes over time in Japanese women's average age at first marriage, average life expectancy and 4-year university enrolment rate. In addition, Figure 1.1 shows trends in Japanese women's total fertility rate and divorce rate.

Women's average age at first marriage increased during the period from the Second World War to the 2000s. During the 50-year period from 1955 to 2005, the average age at first marriage increased by 4.2 years from 23.8 to 28.0 years. This suggests that women now have time before marriage to develop careers in the labour market.

Table 1.1 Average age at first marriage, average life expectancy and 4-year university rate for Japanese women, 1955 to 2005

	Women's average age for first marriage	Women's average life expectancy	Women's 4-year university enrolment rate (%)
1955	23.8	67.8	2.4
1965	24.5	72.9	4.6
1975	24.7	76.9	12.7
1985	25.5	80.5	13.7
1995	26.3	82.9	22.9
2005	28.0	85.5	36.8

Sources: Ministry of Health, Labour and Welfare, Japan, *Heisei 26 nen kani seisei hyō no gaikyō* (Overview of abridged life table 2014) (2015a) (http://www.mhlw.go.jp/toukei/saikin/hw/life/life14/index.html); Ministry of Health, Labour and Welfare, Japan, *Heisei 27 nen waga kuni no jinkō dōtai* (Demographics of Japan 2015) (2015b) (http://www.mhlw.go.jp/toukei/list/dl/81–1a2.pdf); Ministry of Education, Culture, Sports, Science, and Technology (MEXT), Japan, *Gakkō kihon chōsa* (School Basic Survey), various years (http://www.mext.go.jp/b_menu/toukei/chousa01/kihon/1267995.htm).

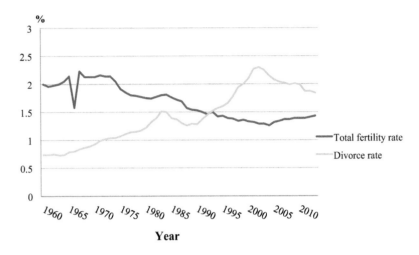

Figure 1.1 Total fertility rate and divorce rate for Japan, 1960 to 2013.

Source: Ministry of Health, Labour and Welfare, Japan, *Heisei 27 nen waga kuni no jinkō dōtai* (Demographics of Japan 2015) (2015b) (http://www.mhlw.go.jp/toukei/list/dl/81–1a2.pdf).

Longer life expectancy and lower fertility can also allow women to develop careers in the labour market. The life expectancy of Japanese women was 67.8 years in 1955, and it continually increased thereafter, surpassing 80 years in the mid-1980s and reaching 86.8 years in 2014.

The total fertility rate was over 4 births per women in the baby-boom era that followed the Second World War, but this fell dramatically in the 1950s and continued to further decline, even after falling below 2 births per women in 1975. In 2013, the total fertility rate was only 1.43 births per women. This suggests that the time Japanese women spend on child rearing has continued to decrease, providing them enough time to participate in the labour market both before and after child rearing.

Moreover, with the popularisation of higher education, women can now accumulate human capital and therefore have a higher likelihood of receiving higher reward in the labour market. In 1955, only 2.4% of women enrolled in a 4-year university course, but that percentage increased to 4.6%, 12.7%, 13.7%, 22.9%, 36.8% and 47.0% in 1965, 1975, 1985, 1995, 2005 and 2014, respectively. In addition, 1975 revealed a large gap between the percentages of men and women enrolled in 4-year university courses: 41.0% for men and 12.7% for women. After 35 years, the gap decreased, with figures of 56.4% for men and 45.2% for women in 2010.

An increase in the divorce rate should also push women into the labour force. The divorce rate in Japan remained low until the 1980s. In 1960, 1970 and 1980, respectively, the rate was 0.74, 0.93 and 1.22 divorces per 1000 population. However, the rate began to increase rapidly during the 1990s, reaching 1.60, 2.10 and 1.84 divorces per 1000 population in 1995, 2000 and 2013, respectively. The divorce rate in Japan in 2010 was at the same level as in France, the Netherlands, Singapore and Korea.

In this way, Japanese society, like other industrialised societies, has some factors that should promote women's entry into the labour market. Why, then, do women with children remain a small part of the labour force? The reasons for this lie in the structure of the Japanese labour market. As discussed by Brinton, Lee and Parish (1995), the effect that women's supply of labour has on their employment is conditioned by labour demand. In other words, interaction between supply and demand for labour – that is, the mechanism of the labour market structure – determines women's employment.

The firm-specific internal labour market and its employment practices

The Japanese labour market is characterised by its firm-specific internal labour market, which was first formed around 1920, and became established in the period of rapid economic growth which began in the 1950s and ended in the early 1970s. Core workers in the firm-specific internal labour market were expected to acquire firm-specific skills through on-the-job training and personnel relocations. A guarantee of lifetime employment and seniority-based wages encouraged core workers to stay with their employers. At the same time, they were expected to show their loyalty to their employers in return for such benefits. Therefore, employees prioritised work over themselves and family demands, and they had to accept overtime work and transfers requiring a change of residence.

However, this way of working is not compatible with the lives of women with children. Accordingly, women who work for large firms or who have white-collar jobs are more likely to resign upon marriage or childbirth because these employment practices are dominant in such workplaces. Moreover, employers refrain from hiring women and bringing them into the firm-specific internal market in anticipation of their resignations. Therefore, parents, anticipating such gender-discriminative employment practices, cut back on their educational investments in their daughters. Brinton (1993) observed that this in turn contributes to limiting women to peripheral roles in the labour market.

Furthermore, women who have exited the firm-specific internal labour market can re-enter the labour market only as non-regular employees, such as part-time workers. This type of employment allows them to work shorter hours, but comes with few benefits. Since the firm-specific internal labour market assumes the hiring of new graduates, those who have exited the market are unable to return to the same positions. Therefore, opportunities for women to return to a position that provides benefits commensurate with their qualifications greatly decrease upon their resignation from a position they held before marriage or childbirth. The size of the penalty paid by women who exit the labour market and the poor working conditions of part-time workers have made it difficult for women with children to obtain jobs that provide benefits commensurate with their qualifications.

Research questions

Japan's severe economic recession during the 1990s and early 2000s greatly influenced the structure of the country's labour market. This book's purpose is to clarify how changes in the Japanese labour market during these periods have affected the employment of women with children.

As will be discussed in Chapter 3, the number of regular employees has decreased and the number of non-regular employees has greatly increased since the 1990s. Therefore, the firm-specific internal labour market is shrinking, and entry into it has become more competitive. Even so, its employment practices remain the same.

On the other hand, along with the declining birth rate in Japan, various social policies were implemented in the 1990s to encourage the employment of women. The Childcare Leave Act of 1991 was amended and improved multiple times through the early 2000s. While the quality of child day-care centres has been threatened, attempts have been made to increase their numbers through substantial deregulation of establishment standards and the establishment of private centres.

This book examines effects of changes in the labour market and social policies on women's employment. Social policies that support women's employment have been argued to facilitate women's entry into the labour market (Gornick, Meyers and Ross, 1997). However, effects of social policies can differ depending on the structure of the labour market where they are introduced (Estévez-Abe, 2007). This book examines how social policies introduced after the 1990s and the labour market structure have interactively influenced women's employment in Japan.

Targeted cohorts and their characteristics

This book examines mainly the employment of women born in the 1960s and 1970s. Many women in these birth cohorts experienced childbirth and child rearing during the 1990s and early 2000s. Figure 1.2 shows social

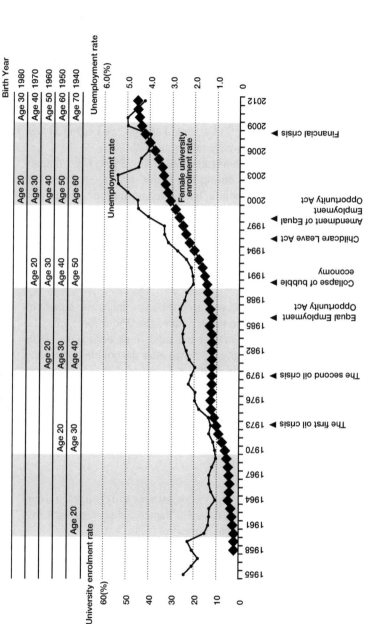

Figure 1.2 Social and economic events in Japan, women's 4-year university enrolment rate, the total unemployment rate and life course of each birth cohort.

Sources: Statistics Bureau, Ministry of Internal Affairs and Communications, Japan, Various years, *Rōdōryoku chōsa* (Labour Force Survey) (http://www.stat.go.jp/data/roudou/2.htm). Ministry of Education, Culture, Sports, Science, and Technology (MEXT), Japan, *Gakkō kihon chōsa* (School Basic Survey), various years, (http://www.mext.go.jp/b_menu/toukei/chousa01/kihon/1267995.htm).

and economic events in Japan, women's 4-year university enrolment rate, the total unemployment rate and the life course of each cohort. As shown in the Figure 1.2, 1960s birth cohort members were born during the period of high economic growth and entered the labour market during the economic recovery of the 1980s. The Equal Employment Opportunity Act for Men and Women was legislated soon after this cohort entered the labour market. Then, the economic bubble burst and a recession hit Japan. At the time, these women were in their early thirties, the time when they were likely engaged in child rearing. Moreover, the Child Care and Family Care Leave Act was implemented while many of them were raising their children.

Members of the 1970s birth cohort turned 20 in the 1990s. The women's 4-year university enrolment rate during this period was about 15%. The economy was hit hard after the bubble burst, around the time when these women completed their educations and were about to enter the labour market. The Child Care and Family Care Leave Act had been enacted by the time they were beginning to have and raise children. However, this period – the early 2000s – was also known as the period of 'the economic recovery that wasn't felt', and the unemployment rate remained high. The real-life economic situation was still grim.

The 1960s and 1970s birth cohorts faced different economic situations after graduation. Those born in the 1960s entered the labour force amid the booming economy of the 1980s. On the other hand, those born in the 1970s did so when the economy drastically worsened after the bubble burst. Nevertheless, the social policies of the 1990s and onward that would support women's employment were enacted when members of both these cohorts gave birth and were raising their children in a bad economy. This book analyses similarities and differences between the effects that socio-economic circumstances had on these women's employment behaviour.

Structure of the book

The M-shaped curve is often mentioned when patterns and changes in women's employment behaviour are discussed. Chapter 2 discusses what this M-shaped curve means and also what it does not mean.

To provide a theoretical framework for explaining the pattern of Japanese women's employment, Chapter 3 discusses the firm-specific internal labour market and the development of social policies. Trends in the labour market under the sluggish economy after the 1990s and their effects on women's employment are discussed. In addition, the chapter discusses the mutual effects of the labour market and social policies to support women's employment in the 1990s and their expected effects on women's employment.

The trends of women's employment after marriage and childbirth are described in Chapter 4. By examining existing survey data and analytical results from the Japanese Panel Survey of Consumers (JPSC), the chapter discusses changes in women's employment rate at marriage and at first childbirth for the 1940s to 1970s birth cohorts.

Chapter 5 examines the dynamics of women's employment during the period of childbirth and child rearing. Building upon existing findings regarding employment of women born from the 1940s to the 1970s, the chapter analyses determining factors in women's employment during three time periods: from 2 years before the birth of their first child up to the year of birth, at 1 year after the birth of their first child and during the decade after the birth of their first child.

Women's re-entry into the labour market and employment patterns after their first childbirth are examined in Chapter 6. The chapter examines not only re-entry into the labour market but also changes in women's employment status after re-entering the labour force. Furthermore, the risk of exit from the labour force among women who were employed at the time of their first childbirth is explored.

Chapter 7 examines the working careers of single mothers. In particular, it examines changes in single mothers' employment status over a certain period and the risk of their exit from the labour force, as well as possible changes to their regular employment.

Chapter 8 summarises results from data analyses in this study and discusses how the labour market structure and social policies during the 1990s and 2000s interactively influenced employment behaviour of Japanese women born in the 1960s and 1970s. After that, some suggestions are put forward for changing women's employment during the child-rearing years, and the prospects for change are addressed.

Data

Data from the Japanese Panel Survey of Consumers (JPSC), conducted from 1993 to 2008 (the survey's first to sixteenth wave), were used for the analyses in this study. The JPSC has been conducted by the Institute for Research on Household Economics since 1993. This panel survey gathers data annually on women from all over Japan who were aged from 24 to 34 years in 1993 (born between 1959 and 1969). Women born during the periods from 1970 to 1973, 1974 to 1979 and 1980 to 1984 were added in 1997, 2003 and 2008, respectively. The present study mainly analyses data of women born in the 1960s and 1970s because by 2008, many had experienced childbirth and begun child rearing.

References

Brewster, Karin L., & Ronald R. Rindfuss. 2000. Fertility and women's employment in industrialized nations. *Annual Review of Sociology*, 26: 271–296.

Brinton, Mary C. 1993. *Women and the economic miracle: Gender and work in postwar Japan.* Berkley: University of California Press.

Brinton, Mary C., Yean-Ju Lee, & William L. Parish. 1995. Married women's employment in rapidly industrializing societies: Examples from East Asia. *American Journal of Sociology*, 100(5): 1099–1130.

Estévez-Abe, Margarita. 2007. Gendering the varieties of capitalism: Gender bias in skills and social policies. In Frances McCall Rosenbluth (Ed.), *The political economy of Japan's low fertility* (pp. 63–86). Stanford: Stanford University Press.

Gornick, Janet C., Marcia K. Meyers, & Katherin E. Ross. 1997. Supporting the employment of mothers: Policy variation across fourteen welfare states. *Journal of European Social Policy*, 7(1): 45–70.

Ministry of Education, Culture, Sports, Science, and Technology (MEXT), Japan. Various years. *Gakkō kihon chōsa* (School Basic Survey). Retrieved from http://www.mext.go.jp/b_menu/toukei/chousa01/kihon/1267995.htm (accessed August 31, 2015).

Ministry of Health, Labour and Welfare, Japan. 2015a. *Heisei 26 nen kani seimei hyō no gaikyō* (Overview of abridged life table 2014). Retrieved from http://www.mhlw.go.jp/toukei/saikin/hw/life/life14/index.html (accessed August 31, 2015).

Ministry of Health, Labour and Welfare, Japan. 2015b. *Heisei 27 nen waga kuni no jinkō dōtai* (Demographics of Japan 2015). Retrieved from http://www.mhlw.go.jp/toukei/list/dl/81–1a2.pdf (accessed August 31, 2015).

OECD. 2011. *Doing better for families: Families are changing.* Paris: OECD.

OECD. 2012. *Closing the gender gap: Act now.* Paris: OECD.

Statistics Bureau, Ministry of Internal Affairs and Communications, Japan. 2015. *Heisei 24 nen shūgyō kōzō kihon chōsa no kekka gaiyō tou* (Results and summary of Employment Status Survey 2012 and former surveys). Retrieved from http://www.stat.go.jp/data/shugyou/2012/index2.htm#kekka (accessed July 3, 2015).

Statistics Bureau, Ministry of Internal Affairs and Communications, Japan. Various years. *Rōdōryoku chōsa* (Labour Force Survey). Retrieved from http://www.stat.go.jp/data/roudou/2.htm (accessed July 29, 2015).

Sundström, Marianne. 1997. Managing work and children: Part-time work and the family cycle of Swedish women. In Hans-Peter Blossfeld & Catherine Hakim (Eds.), *Between equalization and marginalization: Women working part-time in Europe and the United States of America* (pp. 272–288). New York: Oxford University Press.

Vlasblom, Jan Dirk, & Joop J. Schippers. 2004. Increases in female labour force participation in Europe: Similarities and differences. *European Journal of Population*, 20: 375–392.

Yu, Wei-hsin. 2009. *Gendered trajectories: Women, work, and social change in Japan and Taiwan.* Stanford: Stanford University Press.

2 Do more women work than before?

What the M-shaped curve implies

The M-shaped curve and its recent change in Japan

Every so often we hear that more women now work outside the home and that we see a greater level of women's advancement in society. Are these statements true in relation to Japan specifically? If not entirely so, in what sense are they true or not true?

Discussions of trends and changes in women's employment often refer to graphs on which women's employment rate for a given year is plotted for different age groups. In the case of Japanese women, these graphs show a shape of M. This M-shaped curve is not, however, observed for many European countries or the United States, where women's employment rate by age group instead shows a trapezoidal shape. As Figure 2.1 shows, the employment rate does not drop for women between 25 and 39 years of age in societies like Sweden and the United States. In contrast, the M-shaped curve is observed in the case of South Korea. The M-shaped curve is thus used as a point of reference in comparisons between women's employment patterns in Japan and other societies.

Figure 2.2 shows Japanese women's employment rate by age group for 1970, 1990 and 2010. The graph shows an M-shaped curve for each year. However, if we pay attention to changes over the 40 years, we see that the dip in the M-shaped curve becomes smaller with time, indicating a rise in the employment rate for women between 25 and 34 years of age. For 2010, the most recent year, the curve starts to show more of a trapezoidal shape. What can we infer from this change in the shape of the M-curve? Between the age of 25 to 34, which corresponds to the dip in the M-shaped curve, many women get married and raise children. The fact that the dip becomes smaller for more recent data seems to suggest that younger generations are more likely to continue working despite experiencing the life-cycle events of marriage, childbirth and child rearing. But this assumption is not supported by the data illustrated in Figure 2.2: the employment rate that the

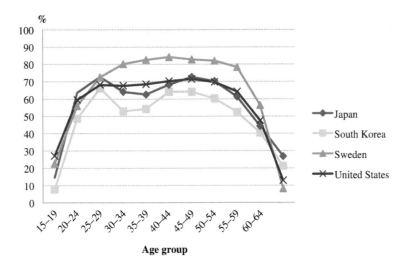

Figure 2.1 Women's employment rate by age groups for Japan, South Korea, Sweden and the United States in 2010.

Sources: Statistics Bureau, Ministry of Internal Affairs and Communications, Japan, *Rōdōryoku chōsa* (Labour Force Survey) for 2010 (http://www.stat.go.jp/data/roudou/2.htm); International Labour Organization, *ILOSTAT Database* for 2010 (http://www.ilo.org/ilostat/faces/home/ statisticaldata?_afrLoop=247784534342474#%40%3F_afrLoop%3D247784534342474%26_ adf.ctrl-state%3Dr92xn3dig_516).

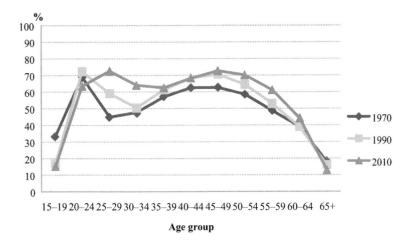

Figure 2.2 Japanese women's employment rate by age groups in 1970, 1990 and 2010.

Source: Statistics Bureau, Ministry of Internal Affairs and Communications, Japan, *Rōdōryoku chōsa* (Labour Force Survey), various years (http://www.stat.go.jp/data/roudou/2.htm).

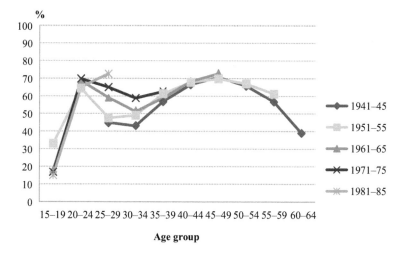

Figure 2.3 Japanese women's employment rate by age groups for different birth cohorts.

Source: Statistics Bureau, Ministry of Internal Affairs and Communications, Japan, *Rōdōryoku chōsa* (Labour Force Survey), various years (http://www.stat.go.jp/data/roudou/2.htm).

Note: Years represent birth cohorts.

women in the 20–24 age group as of 1970 have when they become 40 to 44 years old is not found on the same curve for 1970, but is the value for the 40–44 age group found on the curve for 1990.

Figure 2.3 shows women's employment rate by age group for different birth cohorts. More specifically, for the 1941–1945, 1951–1955, 1961–1965, 1971–1975 and 1981–1985 birth cohorts, the figure shows the employment rate for the 15–19 age group up to the 60–64 age group. Due to data limitations, only employment rates for the 25–29 age group and the older (younger) age groups are available for the 1941–1945 (1981–1985) birth cohort. As Figure 2.3 shows, the dip in the M-shaped curve is smaller for younger cohorts. Although we do not know the employment situation for the 30–34 age group of the 1981–1985 birth cohort, the employment rate for women between 25 and 34 years old rises gradually for the other cohorts (i.e. the 1941–1945 birth cohort to the 1971–1975 birth cohort). (The figure also shows no significant changes in the employment rate for women in their forties for the 1941–1945 birth cohort to the 1961–1965 birth cohort.) We can therefore say that for the 1941–1945 birth cohort to the 1971–1975 birth cohort, the younger the cohort, the larger the proportion of women aged 25 and 34 years with a job.

What this change in the M-shaped curve implies

As mentioned earlier, many women between the ages of 25 to 34 – the age group in which their employment rate rises among younger cohorts – get married and give birth to and raise children. Based on the data shown in Figure 2.3, can we say that younger generations of women are more likely to continue working despite experiencing these life-cycle events? The answer is no. This is because even if the proportion of women who continue working despite these events does not increase, the dip in the M-shaped curve can become smaller for the following reasons.

First, the employment rate for women aged between 25 and 34 can increase due to a tendency for women to marry later in life or not marry at all. According to *Vital Statistics*, published by Ministry of Health, Labour and Welfare of Japan, the average age at first marriage for women has increased, from 24.6 years old in 1970 to 26.9 in 1990 and 29.8 in 2010 (see also Table 1.1 in Chapter 1). Also, calculation based on data from the census reveals that the unmarried rate for women in the 25–29 (30–34) age group has increased from 18.1% (7.2%) in 1970 to 40.2% (13.9%) in 1990 and to 58.9% (33.9%) in 2010. It is possible then that an increase in the proportion of women who delay marriage is raising the employment rate for women aged between 25 and 34.

Second, the dip in the M-shaped curve can become smaller if many women re-enter the labour market more quickly after a short hiatus due to marriage, childbirth or child rearing. In other words, a shorter hiatus from work and a higher rate of success in re-entering the labour market can also increase the employment rate for women aged between 25 and 34.

So, what we can read from the change in the shape of the M-shaped curve (or the pattern of the employment rate plotted against age groups) is limited. The change indicates that for the 1940s birth cohort to the 1970s birth cohort, the younger the cohort, the larger the proportion of 25- to 34-year-old women with a job. However, we must not conclude from the change in the M-shaped curve that younger generations of women are more likely to continue working despite getting married and having and raising children. The reason is that the employment rate by age group like the one shown in Figure 2.3 does not tell us anything about what types of women have a job among the women in a certain age group of a given birth cohort. Moreover, employment rate data do not provide answers to questions regarding women's careers, such as when women in a given birth cohort left and re-entered the labour market, how long was their hiatus from work and whether there were changes between cohorts in these respects.

The fact that the dip in the M-shaped curve has become smaller can lead to various speculations – for example, that younger generations of women have become more likely to continue working despite marriage, childbirth and child rearing or to build a career through the continuation of work. However, we need to keep in mind that the change in the M-shaped curve does not tell us anything about women's careers, their change or the relationship between continuation of work and life events, such as marriage and childbirth.

This book explains what changed and what did not change in Japanese women's employment for the 1940s birth cohort to the 1970s birth cohort. Detailed analysis is conducted mainly for the 1960s and 1970s birth cohorts, with a focus on what types of women have a job (with consideration given to the relationship with life events, such as marriage and childbirth, as well as work experience, family background and other factors) and how they work (which is characterised by types of employment and occupation and by career patterns, including the timing of leaving and re-entering the labour market and the length of hiatus from work). Based on such analysis, this book explains the relationship between child rearing and work and the role of women in this issue against a backdrop of labour market and social policy changes in Japanese society that have occurred over the past 50 years, and discusses prospects for the future of women's employment in Japanese society.

References

International Labour Organization, 2012. ILOSTAT Database. Retrieved from http://www.ilo.org/ilostat/faces/home/statisticaldata?_afrLoop=247784534342474#%40%3F_afrLoop%3D247784534342474%26_adf.ctrl-state%3Dr92xn3dig_516 (accessed March 27, 2014).

Ministry of Health, Labour and Welfare, Japan. Various years. *Jinkō dōtai tōkei* (Vital Statistics). Retrieved from http://www.mhlw.go.jp/toukei/saikin/hw/jinkou/suii09/index.html (accessed October 23, 2013).

Statistics Bureau, Ministry of Internal Affairs and Communications, Japan. Various years. *Kokusei chōsa* (Census). Retrieved from http://www.stat.go.jp/data/kokusei/2010/index.htm (accessed October 23, 2013).

Statistics Bureau, Ministry of Internal Affairs and Communications, Japan. Various years. *Rōdōryoku chōsa* (Labour Force Survey). Retrieved from http://www.stat.go.jp/data/roudou/2.htm (accessed July 29, 2015).

3   The Japanese labour market and social policy arrangements

In Japan, firm-specific internal labour market and social policy arrangements that are closely related to the labour market structure have influenced women's employment. After describing trends in the Japanese economy and labour supply and demand in post-war Japan, this chapter discusses the development of the firm-specific internal labour market and its changes during the 1990s and early 2000s. Next, the Japanese social policy arrangements that have evolved, corresponding to the development of the firm-specific internal labour market, and women's employment-support policies established after the 1990s are discussed. Finally, the chapter examines how the Japanese labour market and social policies interacted to affect women's employment during the 1990s and early 2000s.

Trends in the Japanese economy and labour supply and demand in the post-war period

As is well known, Japan entered a period of rapid economic growth, after chaotic conditions consequent to losing World War II had been brought under control. In the first half of the 1950s, the Japanese government implemented economic policies intended to promote firms' capital accumulation. These included preferential tax treatment for firms investing in facilities and equipment, loosening of the Antimonopoly Act and low-interest lending from public funds made possible by the establishment of a development bank and other entities. Therefore, investment in facilities and equipment became active around 1955, mainly in the heavy and chemical industries, such as shipbuilding, steel making, electric machinery and petrochemical manufacture. For fiscal year 1956, *Keizai Hakusho* (the Economic White Paper) declared that the Japanese society was no longer in the post-war period, and in 1960, Prime Minister Hayato Ikeda presented a plan to double national income. Through these actions, the Japanese economy maintained a high level of economic growth until roughly the first half of the 1970s.

During the high economic growth period, there was sufficient labour for the industrial sector by virtue of the agricultural sector's shrinkage and the male population's growth from the baby boom after the war.

The early 1970s saw global-scale inflation, and Japan's domestic prices escalated because of the first oil crisis in 1973. In response, severely contractionary policies were pursued – for instance, a drastic hike in the interest rate. Although this brought price increases under control, it also resulted in declining demand and company profits. Then, in 1975, the Japanese economy fell into a recession, which was regarded as the worst since the war's end. As domestic demand stagnated, exports started to become a significant part of the Japanese firms' economic activities. And since Japan began to have trade surpluses in 1976, against a backdrop of worldwide economic stagnation, increased exports from Japan became the target of criticism. As a result, the yen appreciated, making it difficult for the export industry to increase profits and leading to a serious economic downturn in 1977 and 1978. The second oil crisis occurred in 1979, resulting in a recession before the economy could benefit from the full effects of policies for boosting domestic demand, implemented in response to criticism of Japan's trade surpluses.

The labour force's age structure shifted from youthful to older labour by the mid-1970s, because of low birth rates from the late 1950s and increases in life expectancy. During the post-oil-crises recession period, large firms conducted employment adjustment, while retaining employment and wage increases for male core employees, and restrictions on hiring the newly graduated and layoffs of young and middle-aged female employees were implemented.

The recession that followed the second oil crisis had largely ended around 1985. The effect of lower import prices caused by yen appreciation spread widely through the economy, contributing to better company profits. Prices stabilised, and firms innovating in computing and other technologies actively invested in facilities and equipment. The economic boom continued from 1987 to 1989. Since prices were stable, an ultra-low interest rate policy continued over the long term. However, a significant part of loaned funds went into speculative activities in the real estate and stock markets, and as a result, land and stock prices skyrocketed, producing what was later considered a bubble economy.

As stock prices and land prices began to fall in 1990 and 1991, respectively, the bubble economy collapsed. In 1991, the Japanese economy entered a long period of economic stagnation, called the 'lost decade'. Because firms had excessive levels of debt, facilities, equipment and employment, a moderate increase in their activities had scarcely any wider positive economic effect. In 1997, currency depreciation in Thailand triggered the Asian currency crisis. In Japan, bankruptcies of large financial institutions followed the closure of Yamaichi Securities.

The employment situation deteriorated during the 1990s, after the bubble economy collapsed. The unemployment rate was 2.1% in 1990 and peaked to 5.4% in 2002. The employment rate for new graduates also worsened, and people began to use the term 'employment ice age' around 1994. Furthermore, in the 1990s, non-regular employment in the labour market became a topic of discussion. As will be discussed further in this chapter, the proportion of non-regular employees had tended upward since the 1980s and the increase accelerated between 1997 and 2002. In Japan, as of 2009, approximately 30% of all employees were non-regular employees (Cabinet Office, Government of Japan, 2009).

The economy began to recover in 2002. Dubbed 'unperceived' in *Keizai Zaisei Hakusho 2007* (the White Paper on the Economy and Public Finance), this economic recovery was not regarded by many as a real recovery. Several possible factors were suggested to be responsible: a relatively moderate pace of economic growth; negligible rises in wages and prices; and little increase in personal consumption because the rise in company profits did not benefit households. Economic recovery continued until 2007. However, the Japanese economy turned downward again, affected by the 2008 collapse of Lehman Brothers and the subsequent global financial crisis. (In this section, the description of trends in the Japanese economy is based on Cabinet Office, Government of Japan, 2009; Cabinet Office Economic and Social Research Institute and Komine, 2011a, 2011b; and Nakamura, 1993, 2007.)

The Japanese labour market structure and women's employment

Dominance of large firms in the Japanese economy

Industrial arrangements in post-war Japan made large firms principal actors in the economy. Hamilton and Biggart (1988) argue that two interrelated networks of firms are crucial: one is an enterprise group comprising links among large firms and the other is an enterprise group connecting small and medium-sized firms to a large firm.

Networks of large firms, best known as *gurūpu* or intermarket groups, are modern-day descendants of the pre–World War II *zaibatsu*. These are groups of firms across industrial sectors linked by central banks or by a trading company. Links among large firms enable them to adopt similar employment policies, such as permanent employment practices.

The other type of enterprise group comprises vertical links among major manufacturers and their related subsidiaries, thus, by 1950s, generating a dual structure in the Japanese economy (Nakamura, 1993). A major manufacturing firm subcontracts machining components and product finishing to small and medium-sized firms. This subcontract system became widespread, because on the one hand, the major large firms can indirectly lower labour cost since wages at small and medium-sized firms are generally less than those at large firms. On the other hand, small and medium-sized firms can be technically guided and financially accommodated by the major firm. Under this system, large firms can increase their use of small firms during times of expansion and decrease their use during times of business decline. Of course, this implies not only that workers at small and medium-sized firms receive lower wages compared with those of large firms but also that their employment is more unstable and vulnerable to economic changes.

These two types of enterprise groups help large firms exert a strong presence in the Japanese economy. Their jointly established employment practices have become 'standard' in Japanese society, although they are incompatible with women's lives, and thus tend to exclude women's employment at large firms.

Development of firm-specific internal labour markets and employment practices

Around the 1920s, large Japanese firms began to create internal labour markets (Odaka, 1984) in part because they needed to actively train newly hired workers to deal with technological innovations that emerged with industrialisation and also because they needed a labour management system under which workers who gained new skills could be retained and would work productively and conscientiously. Seniority-based wage systems resulted and were widely adopted during World War II. After Japan lost the war, the labour market became hierarchical by the 1950s, with three main labour force groups: a regular, core group at large firms working under lifetime employment systems and seniority-based wage systems; a group at small and medium-sized firms, characterised by relatively low wages and high worker turnover; and temporary workers and day workers at small and medium-sized firms and large firms (Nakamura, 1993).

Because only large firms could develop firm-specific internal labour markets, their membership was restricted to core workers working there. What is often called 'Japanese employment practices' – lifetime employment and wages related to the length of service – were applied to them. These practices were institutionalised during and after World War I to reduce high labour turnover and became widespread in the post–World War II period as a response to job scarcity under labour surplus.

Although lifetime employment and seniority-based wage systems are the main features of Japanese employment practices for core workers at large firms, firms also supplemented increasing wages with other inducements, such that workers would remain with the firm. Deferred wages in the form of group insurance and retirement allowances and a system of non-wage welfare benefits conditional on remaining with the firm were roughly introduced parallel with the seniority-based wage systems (Crawcour, 1978). Furthermore, membership in the firm-specific internal labour market and these employment practices are closely related to the recruitment and training system and work culture in large firms. Since the economic growth in the 1960s, large firms have recruited newly graduated, unskilled workers all at once in April, right after their graduation from university. On-the-job training is provided to them, with a series of job rotations, so that they acquire firm-specific skills. This preference for young and inexperienced workers at recruitment and training, jointly conducted by large firms, help to reduce alternative job opportunities for experienced workers. As a result, trained workers tend to stay at the same firm and they climb the occupational ladder within that firm. Furthermore, the firm-specific internal labour market and their employment practices are closely related to a particular work culture among large firms' core workers. That culture includes workers who should show their loyalty to the employer in return for rewards such as long-term job security and wage increases based on length of service. These practices are based on familism, which

> in return for recognition as a member of the 'family', the member was expected to subordinate his individual interests to those of the group and to make himself totally available to the group even to the extent of giving up his life for the group or its head if required.
>
> (Crawcour, 1978, p. 239)

Because of this loyalty, employees feel that they should subordinate their own or family interests to those of the company. Thus, they feel that they cannot refuse to engage in overtime work when needed or to accept relocation assignment irrespective of their family situations.

The impact of firm-specific internal labour markets on women (until the 1980s)

The loyalty required by large Japanese firms is incompatible with most women's lives because they are also responsible for the demands of family.

It is difficult for women to engage in overtime work or to accept a relocation assignment. Thus, it is quite challenging for women to climb the occupational ladder in large firms while raising children. In fact, very few women held managerial positions. In 1989, women in managerial positions in the private sector were at 4.6%, 2.0% and 1.3% for unit chief, section head and manager, respectively (Cabinet Office, Government of Japan, 2013).

Not only do women face difficulty in climbing the occupational ladder, but also they encounter obstacles entering firm-specific internal markets. This is mainly because of 'statistical discrimination', in which an employer seeking to maximise expected profit would discriminate against women (or those with certain ascriptive characteristics) if he believes them to be less qualified, less likely to be long-term and so on as compared to men's averages – particularly under the scarcity of information about the existence and characteristics of workers and jobs (Phelps, 1972). The employer's assumption that women are less qualified and less long-term *on average* is based on previous statistical experience with women and men; women are more likely to quit upon marriage or childbirth. Thus, particularly under the recruitment and training system in the Japanese firm-specific internal labour market, employers have a tendency to hire men compared to women, aiming to avoid loss of training costs they have invested in the newly graduated. In fact, Brinton (1993) observes that in her research conducted in 1984, Japanese men were much more likely than women to start at firm-internal labour market jobs.

Women employed at large firms, but not regarded as core workers, were encouraged not to stay at the firm long. This is called the 'marriage bar' phenomenon (Goldin, 1990); women were implicitly or explicitly encouraged to quit around the time of marriage. Employers benefitted from these women's quitting behaviour, because they were able to replace experienced female employees with younger, inexperienced ones who demanded lower pay. Quitting upon marriage was quite common in Japan. Approximately half of the women born in the 1940s and 1950s (thus, most of whom were anticipated to marry during the 1970s and 1980s) were out of the labour force (see Chapter 4 for more details).

In this way, many women left the labour market upon marriage. However, under the permanent employment and training system in large firms, there were no positions to return to once an employee left the firm. Young female workers not regarded as core workers were always being replaced by younger ones. For those regarded as core workers, quitting means never returning to the same position because core-worker recruiting was mostly limited to new graduates. Thus, most women's careers comprised re-entering the labour market as part-time employees after their children began school. This trend was promoted by 'lean operations' of the Japanese firms during recovery after the oil crises in the second half of the 1970s and early 1980s, when the Japanese firms curbed new hiring and hired part-time employees at low wages.

Notably, in Japan, differences between full-time and part-time employees are a matter of not only working hours but also positions in the labour market. Most part-time jobs are unskilled, dead-end jobs, and firms do not provide training for part-time employees. They seldom have chances for promotion. Consequently, their wages are rather flat, irrespective of their length of service. Their employment contract is short-term, often on a 6-month or yearly basis; therefore, part-time employees are always uncertain of their jobs, even for the near future. Furthermore, they are excluded from non-wage welfare benefits provided by firms, such as housing subsidies, family allowance and company-specific childcare services. The consequences of many middle-aged women taking these jobs are women's unstable employment status and a wide wage gap between men and women. This also indicates lower labour force participation of highly educated, middle-aged women. Because employment opportunities available to them are unattractive, they choose to remain out of the labour force rather than taking less rewarding jobs.

Changes in the Japanese labour market during the 1990s and early 2000s

The Japanese economy suffered a serious downturn during the 1990s and early 2000s. Of course, this affected the labour market, particularly in two ways. First, the number of non-regular employees, including part-time, dispatched, temporary and other types, has increased. According to the Labour Force Survey, the number of non-regular employees was somewhat over 8 million in 1989, and it increased to just over 15.5 million by 2004 (Ministry of Health, Labour and Welfare, Japan, 2015). Percentages of non-regular employees also increased: from 19.1% in 1989 to 31.4% in 2004. In contrast, not only percentages but also the number of regular employees decreased during this period, suggesting that internal labour markets have shrunk and also implying that entrance into the firm-specific internal labour market has become more competitive.

Two employment characteristics should be noted about the increase in non-regular employees during these periods. First, the increase was accompanied by an increase in young, non-regular employees: from 29.2% under age 34 in 1989 to 36.0% in 2004 (Ministry of Health, Labour and Welfare, Japan, 2015). Another characteristic is that non-regular employment has become more diversified, particularly because of the emergence of dispatch workers ('agency workers' or 'temps'). Enacted in 1985 and amended several times, the Worker Dispatch Law was at first limited to professional jobs. However, the types of jobs eligible for dispatch work have gradually enlarged, and in 1999, dispatch work was generally deregulated in response to requests from the industry, where reducing labour cost is an urgent issue. Therefore, Japanese firms began to replace their employees with dispatched workers, particularly in subsidiary clerical and sales jobs, in which many young women were engaged.

The second way that the Japanese economic situation affected the labour market is that, while the internal labour market has decreased, it has persisted, and so have its employment practices. For example, average hours worked per weekday among full-time male employees increased from 1989 to 2006 (Kuroda, 2010), suggesting that core workers' workloads have become heavier and more intensified. Besides, while overall job mobility appears to have increased between the 1950s and early 2000s, mobility among large firms has declined for males. Furthermore, mobility from small and medium-sized firms to large firms has been continuously lower compared to the mobility among large firms (Watanabe, 2011). In brief, entrance barriers to large firms persisted during the 1990s and early 2000s.

The impact of labour market structure on women's employment during the 1990s and early 2000s

The persistent firm-specific internal labour market is supposed to be incompatible with Japanese women meeting the demands of both family and work. As will be discussed more fully in Chapter 4, the percentage of women out of the labour force in the year of their first childbirth is approximately 70% for those born in the 1960s and 1970s, who raised their children during the 1990s and early 2000s. This number is about the same as that of former birth cohorts born in the 1940s and 1950s.

The career-track-based employment management systems that were mainly introduced by large firms, beginning in the mid-1980s and becoming widespread after the 1990s, are not anticipated to change the nature of firm-specific internal labour markets that disadvantage women. In these systems, typically, the firm established two career courses: first, workers with management-track positions who engaged in critical work and potentially experienced job-related relocation; and second, workers with clerical positions who engaged in routine work and had no possibility of relocation. The firm then conducted recruitment activities, provided employee training and made personnel changes based on workers' career courses. Normally, workers in management-track positions were promoted more quickly and could potentially be appointed to managerial positions. In contrast, there were pre-set upper limits to promotions and raises for workers in clerical positions, with no possibility of being promoted to managerial positions. The system itself does not indicate division of female and male; however, many women were encouraged to choose clerical positions because management-track positions could require job-related long-distance relocation. Furthermore, it is rumoured that at job interviews, women who wanted management-track positions were given 'advice' or 'guidance' to choose clerical positions and told about long-distance relocation and other potential difficulties involved in management-track work (Watanabe, 1994).

Even when women obtained management-track positions, they were not necessarily treated equally with male university graduates. A 1991 newspaper article reported cases in which superiors simply told women in management-track positions to visit clients without being taught how to do so. In other cases, women dealt only with small clients while men, hired the same year, were responsible for dealing with large clients (*Asahi Shimbun*, 23 September 1991, morning edition). In other words, firms that introduced career-track-based employment management systems in the 1980s and 1990s probably did not offer management-track women university graduates highly motivating positions or an environment adequate for them to develop job-related skills.

In addition to difficulties of entrance into and career development in the firm-specific internal labour market, the increase in non-regular employment during the 1990s and early 2000s is assumed to make it even more difficult for women to work around the time of childbirth. Not only would non-regular employment impact the lower possibility of marrying (Sasaki, 2012), but also it would affect women's choices in employment when they have children. As previously mentioned, most non-regular jobs in Japan are unskilled and not well paid, thus making women's opportunity cost low. Since the value of women's time for family care is quite high, particularly during early child-rearing years, many women who were engaged in non-regular jobs would quit upon marriage or childbirth. Furthermore, the work–life balance policy, such as childcare leave, often excludes non-regular employees from eligibility, again forcing them out of the labour market. In fact, childcare leave was not applicable for fixed-term employees, in particular, non-regular employees, until 2004, a situation dealt with in detail later in this chapter.

Given these circumstances, this book explores what impact the persistence of firm-specific internal labour market and the increase in non-regular employment will have on women's career choices. It focuses not only on their choices in early child-rearing years but also on the possibility of career development after their children grew somewhat older. However, before examining the labour market structure's impact on women's employment, the following section discusses the Japanese social policy arrangements that closely interact with the labour market and impact women's work–family compatibility as well as their decision to work.

Social policy arrangements and their impacts on women's employment in post-war Japan

Establishment of the 'male breadwinning model' in social welfare

The development of social policy in post-war Japan is closely related to the embeddedness of the firm-specific internal labour market. That is, the male worker in that market is the 'standard' in social policy arrangements. Osawa (2007) calls it 'a system for securing livelihoods based on the male bread-winning model' (p. 54), referring to Esping-Andersen's (1990, 1999) welfare regime theory. Under this system, the labour market is regulated to guarantee that younger middle-aged men have a stable job and earn a wage sufficient to support their wives and children. Given this system, social insurance programs are created to deal with the risk of men losing their earning ability, and wives and children are indirectly covered as dependents of household heads. Wives are expected to perform housework on a full-time basis, and assistance for their work, such as day-care services for children and care services for the elderly, disabled and sick, is provided in exceptional cases (e.g. low income or inability to look after children). The system was created under the slogan 'A Japanese-style welfare society' and was completed around the 1980s.

The most typical example of the male breadwinning model is the social insurance program. Separate programs exist in this regard: employees participate in an employee health insurance program (*kenkō hoken*) and an employee pension program (*kōsei nenkin*), although government employees and private-school personnel participate in their respective mutual aid associations (*kyōsai kumiai*); non-employees participate in a national health insurance program (*kokumin kenkō hoken*) and a national pension program (*kokumin nenkin*). After pension reform in 1985, under the national pension program, participants in the employee pension program or mutual aid pension program were classified as 'Class 2 insured'; participants in the national pension program were classified as 'Class 1 insured'. Furthermore, a new category called 'Class 3 insured' was added to cover dependent spouses (with annual income less than 1.3 million yen) of the Class 2 insured, enabling them to receive basic pensions without making contributions. Creating Class 3 insured involves preferential treatment for couples comprising a salary man and full-time housewife, because contributions of Class 3 insured are substantially paid by all Class 1 and Class 2 insured, including single persons and dual-earner couples. Furthermore, under this system, because spouses of Class 2 insured are regarded as dependent if their annual income is less than 1.3 million yen, many married women try to limit their work hours so that their income does not exceed the upper limit for eligibility of Class 3 insured. If the wife's income exceeds the upper limit and she makes contributions, the household net income becomes lower than when the wife's income is under the upper limit, unless the wife earns far beyond the limit. Thus, the existing Class 3 insured category leads women's careers in certain directions: either remaining a full-time housewife or working shorter hours in lower-paid jobs.

In summary, then, from the period of rapid economic growth to the 1980s, Japan's social policies were based on the premise of men's stable employment at large firms. The policies emphasised that not the government but families, particularly women, were responsible for people's welfare. Notably, the system for securing livelihoods based on the male breadwinning model did not significantly change in the 1990s (Osawa, 2007).

Development of women's employment-support policies since the 1990s

Because of declining birth rates and foreign pressure over gender equality, since the 1990s, the Japanese government has enacted some policies aiming at gender equality and supporting balance between work and family. This section covers three policies that most impact women's employment: the Equal Employment Opportunity Act, the Childcare and Family Care Leave Act and the amendment to the Child Welfare Act.

Equal Employment Opportunity Act

The Equal Employment Opportunity Act was enacted and implemented in 1985 and 1986, respectively, which is around the time that social insurance programs based on the premise of men working at large firms were established. Some state that the law was passed partly because the absence of laws and regulations prohibiting sex discrimination with regard to (non-wage-related) general working conditions was seen as a violation of the Convention on the Elimination of All Forms of Discrimination against Women when Japan was going to ratify it in 1985. The enactment was considered symbolically significant. Simultaneously, many limitations of the law were identified (Osawa, 2002). For example, although the law prohibited discrimination against women with regard to retirement age and firing, it merely required employers to make efforts towards equal treatment in recruitment advertisement, hiring, position assignment and promotion. Furthermore, the then Ministry of Labour notified employers that making something available only to women was lawful as long as it did not compromise the welfare of female workers. Therefore, many firms recruited only women for clerical positions, while they recruited both men and women for management-track positions, which led to wide adoption of career-track-based employment systems.

The Equal Employment Opportunity Act was amended in 1997, 12 years after its enactment. The amended law prohibits discrimination against women in various aspects of employment – recruitment advertisement, hiring, position assignment, promotion, education and training, benefits, retirement age, resignation and firing. Furthermore, in principle, it bans firms from recruiting only women for certain positions, which was previously lawful. Employers are also required to take measures to prevent sexual harassment in the workplace.

Childcare Leave Act

The '1.57 shock' of 1990[1] was a turning point, and declining birth rates began to be considered a problem in various discussions. As a countermeasure, the Japanese government enacted the Childcare Leave Act in 1991. In 1995, the government included stipulations on family care leave and enacted the Childcare and Family Care Leave Act. All businesses were required to allow childcare leave, and childcare leave benefits would be provided from the government's unemployment insurance program. The law was amended in 2001, 2004 and 2009. The 2001 amendment included the prohibition of unfavourable treatment related to such leave and raised the age limit of children for whom workers' shorter hours or other arrangements are allowed, from less than 1 year of age to less than 3 years. The 2004 amendment extended the right to childcare leave to fixed-term employees and made it possible for workers to extend the length of leave (so that they can look after their children until the age of 18 months, instead of the previously set 1-year limitation) if certain conditions were met, such as inability to find a place at a day-care centre by the age of 1 year. The 2009 amendment required employers to institute shorter working hours (e.g. making normal working hours 6 hours per day) for workers raising children younger than 3 years and not to assign overtime work if requested by such workers. The amendment also stipulates that if both parents take childcare leave, the length of the leave can be extended up to 1 year, but not beyond the point when their child becomes 14 months old.

Since 1995, childcare leave benefits have been paid from the unemployment insurance program. When benefits were instituted in 1995, payments were 25% of wages received just before the start of childcare leave. The percentage was raised to 40% in 2001, and then to 50% in 2007. Until 2010, benefits comprised basic childcare leave benefits and reinstatement benefits paid after workers' return to work. For example, for the 50% benefit rate that began in 2007, 30% corresponds to basic benefits and 20% to reinstatement benefits. In 2010, both types of benefits began to be paid during leave. Furthermore, in 2014, the benefit rate for childcare leave has increased to 67% for the first 6 months.

It should be noted that although fixed-term employees (most of them are non-regular employees) became eligible for taking childcare leave according to the 2004 amendment, when the increased number of non-regular employees became more of an issue, it still seemed difficult for non-regular employees to take childcare leave. The Japan Institute for Labour Policy and Training (JILPT, 2011) reports that the percentage of women who took childcare leave among university graduates who were non-regular employees before childbirth was only 9.5% in research conducted in 2010; the percentages are even lower for those who attained less education: 3.4% and 4.1% for high school graduates and junior college graduates, respectively. Women who were non-regular employees before childbirth tend not to take childcare leave if they continue working after childbirth. This occurs partly because the 2004 amendment qualified fixed-term employees to take childcare leave if they are assured employment after returning from leave. However, since many non-regular positions are based on rather short fixed-term contracts, such as 6 months or 1 year, obtaining assurance from the employer for continuous employment is not so simple. Thus, the policy arrangement for using childcare leave reflects the disparity between regular and non-regular employees, in that it creates yet another obstacle for women in non-regular employment to manage the demands of work and family.

Amendment to the Child Welfare Act

The 1997 amendment to the Child Welfare Act brought changes to day-care programs. Under the traditional assistance-based system, municipalities determined whether families who wanted to use day-care centres were actually unable to look after their children. That is, municipalities made discretionary decisions concerning whether families could use services or which facilities could provide services. The 1997 amendment led to the creation of a mechanism through which parents can first obtain sufficient information on various day-care centres and choose those in which to enrol their children, then apply for enrolment, and sign a contract with their municipalities regarding the use of a day-care centre (Jidō Fukushi Hōki Kenkyūkai, 1999). Furthermore, along with the amendment's implementation, the government created a system that would enable all day-care centres to accept infants, reviewed projects so that day-care centres could voluntarily provide extended-hour services and temporary services and made more flexible rules on the number of children enrolled and hours of operation. Furthermore, *Kōsei Hakusho* (the White Paper on Health and Welfare) for fiscal 1998 stated that public day-care centres were less likely to provide diverse services, and thus established their privatisation as a step towards providing such diversity. With an internal notice issued in 2000 by the then Ministry of Health and Welfare, the creation of day-care centres, to that point done by social welfare corporations, was allowed for other entities, and joint-stock companies began entering the day-care business.

Thus, the government's policy direction included more flexibility in day-care programs, relevant deregulation and users' selection of day-care centres; however, simultaneously, some concerns were raised. For example, after an internal notice was issued in 1969 by the then Ministry of Health and Welfare, rooms used for unweaned children had to meet a minimum size standard of 5 m² per child. However, an internal notice issued in 2001 loosened facility requirements for day-care centres, allowing them to accept unweaned children as long as they had separate rooms for them. Furthermore, an internal notice in 1998 permitted creation of branch facilities, which were not mentioned at all in minimum standards, thereby allowing creation of day-care centres without a kitchen, first-aid room, visiting doctor or cook, as required by minimum standards. These deregulations have been identified as de facto dilution of minimum requirements for creation and operation of day-care centres, which had been implemented in 1948 (Tamura, 2004).

Although notably, as of 1997, the law explicitly mentioned users' selection of day-care centres, in reality, the existing system did not have sufficient resources to accommodate such selection in the first place because some regions did not have enough day-care centres. In urban areas particularly, the number of children needing day-care services has exceeded the supply, and resulting waiting lists are an issue. Despite the 2001 Cabinet decision aiming for zero waitlisted children, the problem persists.

Understated effect of women's employment support policies on their employment?

Although the supply of day-care centres is not adequate and the quality of day-care services is threatened, the Japanese government's provision of childcare is evaluated as generous compared with that of the United States and other liberal market economies (Rosenbluth, 2007). However, the impact of social policy on women's employment depends on the welfare regime and particularly on the labour market structure (Estévez-Abe, 2007; Stier, Lewin-Eptein and Braun, 2001). Japanese firm-specific internal labour markets, in which firms hire generalists with the expectation of lifetime employment and on-the-job training, are a type of labour market in which women are particularly disadvantaged. If women plan to interrupt their careers to tend to family needs in the future, acquisition of firm-specific skills is jeopardised, resulting in women's lower earnings and employers' unwillingness to give women the opportunity to acquire firm-specific skills (Estévez-Abe, 2007). Therefore, the effect of certain women's employment support policies – for example, extending the length of childcare leave – on enhancing women's employment is anticipated to be rather limited because these policies do not recover interruption of women's skill acquisition. With these points in mind, this book investigates how women's employment support policies, developed during the 1990s and the early 2000s, interacted with the labour market and affected women's employment patterns.

Note

1 The total fertility rate was 1.57 in 1989. Since this value was lower than the 1.58 observed in 1966 when the birth rate plunged because of *hinoeuma* (a year considered ill-omened for giving birth), it reminded society of declining birth rates' reality.

References

Brinton, Mary C. 1993. *Women and the economic miracle: Gender and work in postwar Japan.* Berkley: University of California Press.

Cabinet Office Economic and Social Research Institute and Takao Komine (Eds.). 2011a. *Nihon keizai no kiroku: dainiji sekiyu kiki heno taiō kara baburu hōkai made* (Report on the Japanese economy: From measures toward the second oil crisis to collapse of bubble economy). Oita: Saeki Printing.

Cabinet Office Economic and Social Research Institute and Takao Komine (Eds.). 2011b. *Nihon keizai no kiroku: kinyū kiki, defure to kaifuku katei* (Report on the Japanese economy: Financial crisis, deflation and process of recovery). Oita: Saeki Printing.

Cabinet Office, Government of Japan. 2009. *Keizai zaisei hakusho Heisei 21 nenban* (White paper on the economy and public finance 2009). Tokyo: Author. Retrieved from http://www5.cao.go.jp/keizai3/keizaiwp/ (accessed March 3, 2014).

Cabinet Office, Government of Japan. 2013. *Danjo kyōdō sankaku hakusho Heisei 25 nenban* (White paper on gender equality 2014). Tokyo: Author. Retrieved from http://www.gender.go.jp/about_danjo/whitepaper/h25/zentai/index.html#pdf (accessed July 29, 2015).

Crawcour, Sydney. 1978. The Japanese employment system. *The Journal of Japanese Studies*, 4(2): 225–245.

Esping-Andersen, Gøsta. 1990. *The three worlds of welfare capitalism.* Princeton, NJ: Princeton University Press.

Esping-Andersen, Gøsta. 1999. *Social foundations of postindustrial economies.* Oxford: Oxford University Press.

Estévez-Abe, Margarita. 2007. Gendering the varieties of capitalism: Gender bias in skills and social policies. In Frances McCall Rosenbluth (Ed.), *The political economy of Japan's low fertility* (pp. 63–86). Stanford: Stanford University Press.

Goldin, Claudia. 1990. *Understanding the gender gap: An economic history of American women.* New York: Oxford University Press.

Hamilton, Gary G., & Nicole Woolsey Biggart. 1988. Market, culture, and authority: A comparative analysis of management and organization in the Far East. *American Journal of Sociology,* 94 Supplement: s52–s89.

The Japan Institute for Labour Policy and Training (JILPT). 2011. *Ikujiki no shūgyō keizoku* (Work continuation in childcare stage). Tokyo: JILPT.

Jidō Fukushi Hōki Kenkyūkai (Ed.). 1999. *Saishin jidō fukushihō boshi oyobi kafu fukushihō boshi hokenhō no kaisetsu* (Commentary on the newest Child Welfare Act, Act for the Welfare of Fatherless Families and Widows, and Maternal and Child Health Act). Tokyo: Jiji Press.

Kuroda, Sachiko. 2010. Do Japanese work shorter hours than before? Measuring trends in market work and leisure using 1976–2006 Japanese time-use survey. *Journal of the Japanese and International Economics,* 24: 481–502.

Ministry of Health, Labour and Welfare, Japan. 2015. *Hiseiki koyō no genjō to kadai* (Current conditions and agenda on non-regular employment). Retrieved from http:// www.mhlw.go.jp/stf/seisakunitsuite/bunya/0000046231.html (accessed July 28, 2015).

Ministry of Health and Welfare, Japan. 1998. *Kōsei hakusho heisei 10 nendo ban* (White paper on health and welfare 1998). Tokyo: Gyosei.

Nakamura, Takafusa. 1993. *Nihon keizai: Sono seichō to kōzō* (The Japanese economy: Its development and structure). 3rd edition. Tokyo: University of Tokyo Press.

Nakamura, Takafusa. 2007. *Shōwa keizaishi* (The economic history of Showa era). Tokyo: Iwanami Shoten.

Odaka, Konosuke. 1984. *Rōdō shijō bunseki* (Analysis on labour market). Tokyo: Iwanami Shoten.

Osawa, Mari. 2002. *Danjo kyōdō sankaku shakai wo tsukuru* (Building a gender equal society). Tokyo: Nippon Hōsō Kyōkai.

Osawa, Mari. 2007. *Gendai nihon no seikatsu hoshō shisutemu* (The system for securing livelihoods in contemporary Japan). Tokyo: Iwanami Shoten.

Phelps, Edmund S. 1972. The statistical theory of racism and sexism. *The American Economic Review,* 62(4): 659–661.

Rosenbluth, Frances McCall (Ed.). 2007. *The political economy of Japan's low fertility.* Stanford: Stanford University Press.

Sasaki, Takayuki. 2012. Fukakujitsu na jidai no kekkon (Marriage at a time of uncertainty). *Japanese Journal of Family Sociology,* 24(2): 152–164.

Stier, Haya, Noah Lewin-Eptein, & Michael Braun. 2001. Welfare regimes, family-supportive policies, and women's employment along the life-course. *American Journal of Sociology,* 106(6): 1731–1760.

Tamura, Kazuyuki. 2004. *Hoikusho no mineika* (Privatisation of day-care centres). Tokyo: Shinzansha.

Watanabe, Takashi. 1994. Kōsu betsu kanri to danjo kyōdō wo meguru shomondai (The career-track-based employment management systems and issues in gender equality). In Takashi Watanabe & Tsuyako Nakamura (Eds.), *Danjo kyōgyō no shokuba zukuri* (Forming gender-equal workplace) (pp. 92–128). Kyoto: Minerva Shobo.

Watanabe, Tsutomu. 2011. Shokureki kara miru koyō no ryūdōka to koteika (Mobilization and immobilization of employment viewed from work career). In Hiroshi Ishida, Hiroyuki Kondo, & Keiko Nakao (Eds.), *Gendai no kaisō shakai 2* (The contemporary stratification society, 2) (pp. 173–187). Tokyo: University of Tokyo Press.

4 Marriage, childbirth, child rearing and women's employment

Among women who have experienced childbirth and child rearing, has the percentage who continued to work through that period of their lives increased? Based on previous findings from several long-term, nationwide samples gathered by the government, research institutes and research groups on women's employment, this chapter examines changes in the employment behaviour of women who have experienced marriage, childbirth and child rearing. Many of these surveys use the same or relatively similar questions and ask women in a certain age group at the time of the survey to provide their responses. In such studies, different birth cohorts are included in each survey. For example, if studies are conducted in different years, the employment behaviour of women in their thirties actually corresponds to that of different birth cohorts. Moreover, the wording of questions on women's employment behaviour and methods of data calculation differ across studies. Hence, numbers derived from these studies, such as the continuous employment rate of women before and after childbirth, can indicate different things across different studies.

This chapter pieces together, as far as possible, findings from different studies and sheds light on women's employment after marriage and childbirth according to birth cohort. In addition, to show how women's continuous employment rate can appear to differ depending on the calculation method used, various methods are employed to derive women's continuous employment rate after marriage and childbirth using the data from the JPSC.

Has the number of women who remain in the labour force after marriage increased?

Employment rate at marriage

Trends in the employment rate at marriage by birth cohort are discussed first. Using the Nationwide Survey on Work and Family Life conducted by the Japan Institute of Labour (JIL; now the Japan Institute for Labour Policy and Training [JILPT]) in 1991, Imada (1996) calculated the employment rate (self-employed workers were excluded from 'employed') at marriage by cohort. Although detailed numbers were not provided in her paper, Imada did provide the following employment rates at marriage: slightly below 50% in the 1942–1946 birth cohort, slightly below 65% in the 1952–1956 birth cohort and slightly over 70% in the 1962–1966 birth cohort.

Furthermore, according to the 12th National Fertility Survey, the employment rate of women after marriage (when they became aware of their first pregnancy for those who had at least one child and when the survey was conducted for those who had not given birth) was 52.8%, 55.7%, 63.2% and 65.1% in the 1952–1954, 1955–1959, 1960–1964 and 1965–1967 birth cohorts, respectively (National Institute of Population and Social Security Research, Japan, 2003).

As for the results from surveys that include data on younger generations of women, according to the 4th National Survey on Family conducted in 2008, the employment rate of women during pregnancy with their first child – not at marriage – was 44.9%, 56.5%, 60.1%, 67.3% and 73.6% in the 1939–1943, 1949–1953, 1959–1963, 1969–1973 and 1979–1983 birth cohorts, respectively (National Institute of Population and Social Security Research, Japan, 2010).

The Longitudinal Survey of Adults in the 21st Century is an annual survey of adults born from 1968 to 1982 and was first conducted in 2002. According to the 10th survey, the post-marriage employment rate was 68.4% among women who married within 9 years after the start of the survey (calculated from published tables by Ministry of Health, Labour and Welfare, Japan).

The foregoing studies differ slightly from one another due to the selection of different measurements (whether self-employed workers are included) and time points (at marriage, after marriage or during pregnancy with their first child). However, shifts in women's overall employment rate (labour force participation rate) and the pattern of each birth cohort over time are similar among studies. Women's employment rate at marriage (or soon after marriage) was slightly below 50% in the 1940s birth cohort, around 55% in the 1950s birth cohort, slightly above 60% in the 1960s birth cohort and around 70% in the 1970s birth cohort. In other words, the employment rate at marriage was higher in younger cohorts.

Other notable findings from these studies are that a smaller percentage of women in younger cohorts were self-employed or employed in their family businesses and that the percentages of not only regular employees but also non-regular employees were higher in younger cohorts. For example, the 12th National Fertility Survey found that the percentage of women employed in their family businesses after marriage was 9.7%, 8.1%, 6.3% and 4.5% in the 1952–1954, 1955–1959, 1960–1964 and 1965–1967 birth cohorts, respectively. On the other hand, the percentage of women working as regular employees was 32.6%, 34.7%, 39.0% and 41.5%, and the percentage of women working as non-regular employees (part-time, dispatched or contract workers) was 10.5%, 12.9%, 17.9% and 19.1% in the 1952–1954, 1955–1959, 1960–1964 and 1965–1967 birth cohorts, respectively (National Institute of Population and Social Security Research, Japan, 2003).

Continuous employment rate before and after marriage

Data from the 3rd National Survey on Family show that the percentage of women who continued working after marriage was 21.9%, 27.8% and 38.9% in the 1939–1943, 1949–1953 and 1969–1973 birth cohorts, respectively (National Institute of Population and Social Security Research, Japan, 2010).

Using data from the Social Stratification and Social Mobility Survey (SSM) conducted in 1995, Yoshida (2004) calculated women's regular employment continuation rate, operationalised as the percentage of women who continued to hold the same regular employment position at the same workplace 1 year after marriage among those who were regular employees at the time of marriage. Yoshida found that the regular employment continuation rate was higher in younger cohorts: 18.2%, 20.0% and 27.5% in the 1941–1945, 1951–1955 and 1961–1965 birth cohorts, respectively.

Similarly, using data from the 11th National Fertility Survey conducted in 1997, Senda (2002) calculated the percentage of women who were regular employees soon after marriage among those who were regular employees before marriage. It was about 40% in the 1950–1954 birth cohort and 45%–50% in the 1960–1964 birth cohort.

Continuous employment rates by different calculation methods

The continuous employment rate can vary depending on the time frame (a period before marriage until marriage or a period that begins at marriage), type of employment (limited to regular employment or not) and the denominator (the whole target cohort or limited to those who were employed or were regular employees at marriage (or before marriage). To show variations, employment rates are calculated from JPSC data ahead according to different methods.

Data from the JPSC mainly cover the 1960s and 1970s birth cohorts. Among women whose employment status was known in the year of their first marriage and in the years before and after marriage ('marriage' is limited to first marriage), the trend by cohort was observed. Table 4.1 shows that the employment rate in the year of marriage was 63.5% and 67.7% in

Table 4.1 Distribution of employment status around the time of marriage, for the 1960s and the 1970s birth cohorts

	(%)					
	1960s birth cohort (n = 918)			*1970s birth cohort (n = 623)*		
	Previous year of marriage	*The year of marriage*	*The year after marriage*	*Previous year of marriage*	*The year of marriage*	*The year after marriage*
Regular	72.2	45.3	27.8	63.4	45.4	29.4
Non-regular	12.9	12.4	13.2	20.7	19.4	19.6
Self-employed	4.1	5.8	6.0	2.6	2.9	3.7
Not employed	10.8	36.5	53.1	13.3	32.3	47.4
Total	100	100	100	100	100	100

Source: JPSC.

the 1960s and 1970s birth cohorts, respectively. These values are similar to those obtained from other survey data sets discussed earlier. When differences in the breakdown of employment status are considered, the percentage of women who were non-regular employees was higher for the 1970s birth cohort than for the 1960s birth cohort at all three time points considered, before and after marriage. There is not a great difference between the 1960s and 1970s birth cohorts in the percentage of women who were regular employees in the year of marriage and the year after marriage. Therefore, a higher employment rate at marriage in the 1970s cohort than in the 1960s cohort can be attributed to an increase in the percentage of non-regular employees, not regular employees.

Next, the continuous employment rate from the year prior to marriage to the year after marriage is examined. Due to some data limitations, women whose employment status did not change in the years before and after marriage are considered cases of continuous employment.[1] Table 4.2 shows the percentage of women who remained employed and those who continued to be regular employees among all members of each cohort (shown in the first and second rows) and the percentage of women who remained regular employees among those who were regular employees in the previous year (or 2 years before) (shown in the third row). Time frames were as follows: from the year before marriage to the year of marriage; from the year of marriage to 1 year after marriage; from the year before marriage to 1 year after marriage.

The continuous employment rate from the year before marriage to the year of marriage (regardless of employment status) was approximately 60% for both the 1960s and the 1970s birth cohorts. However, rates from the year

Table 4.2 Women's continuous employment rate around the time of the first marriage, for the 1960s and the 1970s birth cohorts

	(%)					
	1960s birth cohort (n=918)			*1970s birth cohort (n=623)*		
	From the year before marriage to the year of marriage	*From the year of marriage to 1 year after marriage*	*From the year before marriage to 1 year after marriage*	*From the year before marriage to the year of marriage*	*From the year of marriage to 1 year after marriage*	*From the year before marriage to 1 year after marriage*
The percentage of women who remained employed among all members of each cohort	60.9	41.9	40.5	62.8	46.7	43.0
The percentage of women who continued to be regular employees among all members of each cohort	43.6	25.7	25.0	40.9	27.4	24.9
The percentage of women who remained regular employees among those who were regular employees in the previous year (or two years before)	60.3	56.7	35.4	64.6	60.4	41.0

Source: JPSC.

of marriage to 1 year after marriage and from the year before marriage to 1 year after marriage were from 40% to 50%. Calculated among all members of each cohort, but limited to regular employees, the regular employment continuation rate from the year before marriage to the year of marriage was approximately 40% for both the 1960s and the 1970s birth cohorts. The rate dropped to less than 30% when it was calculated from the year of marriage to 1 year after marriage, and from the year before marriage to 1 year after marriage. Among women who were regular employees, the regular employment continuation rate from the year before marriage to the year of marriage was over 60% for both the 1960s and the 1970s birth cohorts. The rate from the year of marriage to 1 year after marriage was slightly over 55% and about 60% in the 1960s and 1970s birth cohorts, respectively. The rate from the year before marriage to 1 year after marriage was 35% and about 40% in the 1960s and 1970s birth cohorts, respectively.

Are younger women more likely to continue working after marriage?

Patterns of continuous employment among women before and after marriage are summarised in this section by linking results of data analyses as well as previous findings. The continuous employment rate before and after marriage is slightly higher in younger cohorts, although it does not increase dramatically. The regular employment continuation rate from the year of marriage to 1 year after marriage was a little less than 20% in the 1940s birth cohort. It was slightly higher in the 1960s and 1970s birth cohorts, from 25% to 30%. When non-regular employees were included, the continuous employment rate was much higher in younger cohorts because they had a higher percentage of non-regular female employees. The regular employment continuation rate among women who were regular employees before marriage varied slightly across studies, and this leaves some uncertainty. Nevertheless, the rate is assumed to be from 50% to 60% in the 1950s, 1960s and 1970s birth cohorts. In addition, both the continuous employment rate (regardless of employment status) and the regular employment continuation rate were lower from the year of marriage to 1 year after marriage than from the year before marriage to the year of marriage. This suggests that both the continuous employment rate (regardless of employment status) and the regular employment continuation rate vary greatly depending on the time frame considered.

Put another way, the employment rate of women at marriage was certainly higher in younger cohorts, reaching approximately 70% in the 1970s birth cohort. Yet the regular employment continuation rate from the year of marriage to the year after marriage was only about 25% to 30% in the 1970s birth cohort. In the 1950s, 1960s and 1970s birth cohorts, more than half the women who were regular employees in the year before marriage were no longer regular employees in the year after marriage.

It is sometimes said that younger Japanese women are more likely to remain in the labour force even after marriage. This is wrong, however, if we take it to mean that younger women are more likely to continue to be regular employees after marriage. The percentage of women who are non-regular employees is higher among younger cohorts. Among all members of the 1970s cohort, the regular employment continuation rate from the year of marriage to 1 year after marriage was only about 25% to 30%. Notably, not many women stay in regular employment positions before and after marriage.

Has the number of women who remain in the labour force after childbirth increased?

The difficulty in attributing employment behaviour to either marriage or pregnancy and childbirth

As discussed in the previous section, according to analyses of JPSC data, the continuous employment rate from the year of marriage to 1 year after marriage was much lower than that from the year before marriage to the year of marriage in both the 1960s and 1970s birth cohorts. This might be because of the existing norm in Japan that holds it natural for women to marry and then give birth. If this is the case, investigating whether the employment behaviour of women right after marriage is due to marriage or to pregnancy and childbirth may be meaningless in Japan.

Employment rate after childbirth

Imada (1996) calculated women's employment rates by cohort in the year of first childbirth and 1 year afterwards. The reported employment rate at first childbirth was approximately 20%, approximately 30% and slightly over 40% in the 1942–1946, 1952–1956 and 1962–1966 birth cohorts, respectively. However, the employment rate 1 year after birth was about 15% in the 1942–1946 birth cohort, and the rates in the 1952–1956 and 1962–1966 birth cohorts were around 25%. Although only figures by marriage cohort were reported, Kojima (1995) used data from the 10th National Fertility Survey (targeted cohorts were 1942–1974 birth cohorts) to show that the employment rate during the infancy of a first child was around 25% to 35% and that the regular employment rate during this period was around 10% to 15%. In addition, according to the 12th National Fertility Survey, the employment rate when the first child was 1 year old was 26.1%, 28.7%, 26.7% and 26.4% in the 1952–1954, 1955–1959, 1960–1964 and 1965–1967 birth cohorts, respectively (National Institute of Population and Social Security Research, Japan, 2003). When limited to regular employment rate, the rate becomes 13.3%, 16.7%, 15.8% and 16.6% in these cohorts, respectively. Using data from the Balancing Work with Life study conducted by the JILPT in 2005, Imada and Ikeda (2006) reported that the employment rate of women 1 year after their first childbirth was from 20% to 30% for all cohorts born from 1950 to 1975.

Therefore, the employment rate after first childbirth does not seem to differ much across cohorts born from the 1940s to the 1970s. The employment rate of women 1 year after first childbirth was around 25% to 30% for cohorts born from the 1940s to the 1970s, and their regular employment rate was around 10% to 15%.

Continuous employment rate after childbirth

According to data from the 3rd National Survey on Family (2003), the percentage of women who kept their jobs after the birth of their first child was 17.2%, 19.1%, 16.3% and 18.7% in the 1939–1943, 1949–1953, 1959–1963 and 1969–1973 birth cohorts, respectively (National Institute of Population and Social Security Research, Japan, 2006). Using data from the SSM, Yoshida (2004) examined differences across cohorts in the percentage of women who kept their regular employment position at the same workplace 1 year after childbirth among those who had given birth over 1 year earlier. The results showed that the regular employment continuation rate at childbirth was around 20% for all cohorts born from 1941 to 1965. Moreover, results from the 10th Longitudinal Survey of Adults in the 21st Century, which targeted those born from 1968 to 1982, showed that the continuous employment rate among women who gave birth to a first and only child during the study period was 32.3%. Their regular employment continuation rate was 20.3% (calculated from published tables by Ministry of Health, Labour and Welfare, Japan).

These numbers suggest that the continuous employment rate after first childbirth was around 20% for women born between the 1940s and 1960s. The number was also around 20% when the regular employment continuation rate was considered. This might be because opportunities for continuous employment after childbirth were open only to regular employees.

Employment and continuous employment rates in the 1960s and 1970s birth cohorts before and after childbirth

Data from the JPSC are analysed to examine the employment and continuous employment rates of women born in the 1960s and 1970s before and after giving birth. Here the analysis is limited to employment and continuous employment before and after the birth of the first child, not the second or third.

Table 4.3 shows women's employment status 2 years before and 1 year before the birth of their first child, in the year of the first birth and 1 year after the birth, according to cohort. What should be noted first is that employment rates of the 1960s and 1970s cohorts fell drastically between the 2 years prior to childbirth and the year of birth. Although approximately 80% of women in both cohorts were in the labour force 2 years before the birth,

Table 4.3 Distribution of employment status around the time of birth of their first child, for the 1960s and the 1970s birth cohorts

	(%)							
	1960s birth cohort (n = 852)				*1970s birth cohort (n = 581)*			
	2 years before birth	*1 year before birth*	*The year of birth*	*1 year after birth*	*2 years before birth*	*1 year before birth*	*The year of birth*	*1 year after birth*
Regular	62.7	39.8	19.1	15.9	56.3	40.1	19.1	16.4
Non-regular	15.6	11.2	4.6	6.0	21.7	17.4	6.9	11.2
Self-employed	5.2	6.3	6.3	6.3	2.6	2.9	4.0	4.3
Not employed	16.6	42.7	70.0	71.8	19.5	39.6	70.1	68.2
Total	100	100	100	100	100	100	100	100

Source: JPSC.

the number dropped to approximately 60% 1 year before the birth and to around 30% in the year of the birth. When employment status is considered, something else becomes clear. The regular employment rate fell dramatically from 2 years before the first birth to 1 year after the birth. The regular employment rate for women born in the 1960s and 1970s was around 60% 2 years before the first birth, but fell to around 15% 1 year after the birth. There was not much difference between cohorts, but the percentage of non-regular employees was higher in the 1970s cohort.

Table 4.4 shows the continuous employment rate for those who remained employed and those who remained in regular employment among all women in each cohort. The table also shows the rate for those who remained in regular employment as a percentage of those who were regular employees in the previous year. The time frames are as follows: from 2 years before the first birth to 1 year before the birth, from 1 year before the birth to the year of birth and from the year of the birth to 1 year after the birth. Regardless of employment status, the continuous employment rate among all women (shown in the first row) was from 50% to 60% for both the 1960s and the 1970s birth cohorts from 2 years before the first birth to 1 year before the birth. It dropped to 25% to 30% from 1 year before the first birth to the year of birth. It dropped further, to slightly over 20%, from the year of the first birth to 1 year after the birth. The percentage of women who remained in regular employment, of all women in each cohort (shown in the second row), was from 35% to 40% from 2 years before the first birth to 1 year before the birth in both cohorts. This percentage dropped to slightly below 20% from 1 year before the first birth to the year of birth. It dropped

Table 4.4 Women's continuous employment rate around the time of the first childbirth, for the 1960s and the 1970s birth cohorts

	(%)					
	1960s birth cohort (n=852)			1970s birth cohort (n=581)		
	From 2 years before the first birth to 1 year before the birth	From 1 year before the birth to the year of birth	From the year of the birth to 1 year after the birth	From 2 years before the first birth to 1 year before the birth	From 1 year before the birth to the year of birth	From the year of the birth to 1 year after the birth
Percentage of women who remained employed among all members of each cohort	54.2	28.5	23.9	56.3	25.8	23.8
Percentage of women who continued to be regular employees among all members of each cohort	37.9	18.8	15.0	36.8	17.4	14.5
Percentage of women who remained regular employees among those who were regular employees in the previous year	60.5	47.2	78.5	65.4	43.3	75.7

Source: JPSC.

further, to around 15% from the year of the first birth to 1 year after the birth. For both the 1960s and 1970s birth cohorts, the percentage of women who remained in regular employment out of those who were regular employees in the previous year (shown in the third row) was from 60% to 70% from

2 years before the first birth to 1 year before the birth, from 40% to 50% from 1 year before the first birth to the year of birth, and slightly below 80% from the year of the first birth to 1 year after the birth.

Percentages of women who remained employed and in regular employment of all women in each cohort were not markedly different during two time frames: from the year before the first birth to the year of birth and from the year of the first birth to the year after the birth. This suggests that women who remained in the labour force until the year of the birth of their first child were highly likely to remain in the labour force after the birth. In particular, when the analysis is limited to regular employees, about 80% of women who were regular employees in the year of the first birth continued to be regular employees 1 year after the birth.

However, the continuous employment rate from 1 year before the first birth to the year of birth among all women was only 25% to 30% when all types of employment were considered; the number was slightly below 20% when only regular employment was considered. Table 4.4 suggests that very few women remained in the labour force until the year of birth.

The continuous employment rate remains low

The figures obtained from this and other studies allow for some findings. First, women's employment rate 1 year after their first childbirth was from 25% to 30% for the 1940s to 1970s birth cohorts. The regular employment rate 1 year after their first childbirth for these cohorts was from 10% to 15%. For women born from the 1940s to the 1970s, the continuous employment rate after their first childbirth was 20%, and the regular employment continuation rate was 15% to 20%. Little difference was observed across birth cohorts (1940s and 1970s), although the percentage of women who were non-regular employees was higher in the younger cohorts. The continuous employment rate might be slightly higher in the 1980s birth cohort, but not enough data have yet been collected.

Analysis of the JPSC data suggests that women in the 1960s and 1970s birth cohorts who remained in the labour force after their first childbirth were the few women who could keep their regular employment positions until the year of birth. As shown in Table 4.4, which presents results for the continuous employment rate before and after the first childbirth, around 80% of women who were regular employees in the year of the first birth continued to be regular employees 1 year after the birth. The table also shows that very few women kept their positions as regular employees until the year of the first birth. Women who were regular employees 1 year before birth and remained so in the year of birth made up only slightly less than 20% of each birth cohort. The women who remained in the labour force 1 year after the first birth were the lucky few with employment conditions that allowed them to remain in the labour force as regular employees. On the other hand, a great majority of women had given up continuous employment by the year of birth.

Note

1 Regarding employment history before the beginning of the study period, only a question on employment status at a certain age was asked retrospectively. Therefore, even if women were regular employees prior to the year of marriage and also in the year of marriage, we cannot determine whether they remained at the same workplace throughout the period.

References

Imada, Sachiko. 1996. Joshi rōdō to shūgyō keizoku (Women's work and employment continuation). *The Japanese Journal of Labour Studies*, 433: 37–48.

Imada, Sachiko, & Shingo Ikeda. 2006. Shussan josei no koyō keizoku ni okeru ikuji kyūgyō seido no kōka to ryōritsu no kadai (The effect of childcare leave on women's work continuation after childbirth, and agenda on supporting work-family compatibility). *The Japanese Journal of Labour Studies*, 553: 34–44.

Kojima, Hiroshi. 1995. Kekkon, shussan, ikuji oyobi shūgyō (Marriage, childbirth, child rearing, and employment). In Hiroshi Obuchi (Ed.), *Josei no raifu saikuru to shūgyō kōdō* (Women's life cycle and employment behaviour) (pp. 61–87). Tokyo: Printing Bureau, Ministry of Finance of Japan.

Ministry of Health, Labour and Welfare, Japan. Various years. *21 seiki seinensha jūdan chōsa: heisei 14 nen seinensha* (Longitudinal Survey of Adults in the 21st century: 2002 cohort). Retrieved from http://www.mhlw.go.jp/toukei/list/28–9.html (accessed November 1, 2013).

National Institute of Population and Social Security Research, Japan. 2003. *Heisei 14 nen dai 12 kai shusshō dōkō kihon chōsa dai I hōkokusho* (The first report on 12th National Fertility Survey, 2002). Tokyo: Health and Welfare Statistics Association.

National Institute of Population and Social Security Research, Japan. 2006. *Dai 3 kai zenkoku katei dōkō chōsa no kekka no gaiyō ni tsuite* (Summary of 3rd National Survey of Family). Retrieved from http://www.ipss.go.jp/ps-katei/j/NSFJ3/NSFJ3_top.asp (accessed November 1, 2013).

National Institute of Population and Social Security Research, Japan. 2010. *Dai 4 kai zenkoku katei dōkō chōsa no kekka no gaiyō ni tsuite* (Summary of 4th National Survey of Family). Retrieved from http://www.ipss.go.jp/ps-katei/j/nsfj4/nsfj4_top.asp (accessed November 1, 2013).

Senda, Yukiko. 2002. Kikon josei no shūgyō keizoku to ikuji shigen no kankei (The association between married women's work continuation and childcare resources). *Journal of Population Problems*, 58(2): 2–21.

Yoshida, Takashi. 2004. M ji kyokusen ga sokoageshita hontō no imi (The real meaning in rise the bottom of M-shaped curve). *Japanese Journal of Family Sociology*, 16(1): 61–70.

5 Women's employment during the childbirth and child-rearing years

Human capital, household economic status and social support as major factors

The previous chapter showed that the employment rate before and after marriage and childbirth in the 1960s and 1970s birth cohorts, who experienced childbirth and child rearing from the late 1990s to the early 2000s, were about the same as those in earlier cohorts. This chapter explores the dynamics that hinder women's employment during their childbirth and child-rearing years. In previous studies, women's human capital, household economic status and social support were considered major factors affecting women's employment, and they were often measured by women's educational attainment, husband's income and parents' support, respectively. Accordingly, this chapter examines previous findings on the effects of these factors. Results of data analysis on women's employment in the 1960s and 1970s birth cohorts are then shown. In examination of findings from previous studies, attention is paid to trends by birth cohort to the extent possible.

Educational attainment

From the perspective of human capital theory, women's higher educational attainment should enhance their utility in the labour market and increase their opportunity cost of non-participation in the labour force; therefore, higher educational attainment is expected to facilitate women's employment. However, the effects of higher educational attainment on women's employment during the time around childbirth have not been closely observed in Japan.

Few Japanese studies have found a positive effect of higher educational attainment on employment among women born from approximately the 1920s to the 1960s. Tanaka (1998) analysed SSM data (1985, 1995) with target cohorts born between 1916 and 1975 and concluded that, except for women in teaching positions, higher educational attainment did not have any effect on the continuous full-time employment rate of women in the period between marriage and the birth of their youngest child. In addition, Kojima (1995) examined data from the 10th National Fertility Survey (target cohorts born from 1942 to 1974) and found no effect of university education on full-time employment.

Some studies have found a positive effect of university education on the employment of women born from the 1920s to the 1960s during the early child-rearing years. However, these findings should be viewed with caution for several reasons. For example, Imada (1996) examined the Nationwide Survey on Occupation and Family Life conducted by the JIL (now the JILPT) in 1991 (target cohorts born from 1922 to 1966) and found that, compared with women who were high-school graduates, women who graduated from junior college, vocational college or university were more likely to be employed than be 'not employed'. However, in Imada's study, it is assumed that those who were 'not employed' included those who were self-employed or employed in their family businesses. In Japan, because higher educational attainment is generally believed to be more strongly associated with employed labour than with self-employment or employment in a family business, we cannot safely infer from this finding that women with higher educational attainment are more likely to have a job than to be without a job during their child-rearing years. Similarly, using the Employment Status Survey of 1987 (target cohorts born from 1933 to 1962), Osawa (1993) examined the effect of educational attainment on the likelihood of women being regular employees compared with being outside the labour force, according to age. She found that the years of education enhanced the likelihood of women in the 25 to 29 and 30 to 34 age groups becoming regular employees. Her study's focus was limited to married women, but this would also include married women without children. Therefore, from this analysis, it is difficult to determine the effect of educational attainment on women's employment during the child-rearing years.

On the other hand, many studies on women born from the 1960s to the 1980s have noted a positive effect of higher educational attainment on women's employment during their child-rearing years. Using data from the 11th National Fertility Survey (1997), Senda (2002) analysed the likelihood of women being continuously employed as regular employees during the period between their first pregnancy and 1 year after childbirth, finding a positive effect of years in education for cohorts born after 1959. Nagase (1999) (targeting 1957 to 1975 birth cohorts) and Shintani (1998) (targeting the 1980s marriage cohort) analysed the same survey and also found a positive effect of educational attainment on the likelihood of women being regular employees 1 year after the birth of their first child. A study conducted by Osawa and Suzuki (2000) examined data from the JPSC and found a positive effect of educational attainment on the likelihood of women who gave birth from 1993 to 1996 being continuously employed full-time from 1 year before childbirth to the year of birth.

However, some studies with data on relatively younger cohorts have found no effect of educational attainment on women's employment during the child-rearing years. Imada and Ikeda (2006) analysed data from the Balancing Work with Life study conducted by the JILPT in 2005 (targeting 1950 to 1975 birth cohorts), finding no effect of years of education on the likelihood of women who were employed during the 1-year period before the birth of their first child remaining in the labour force until the birth. Moreover, using data from the 4th National Fertility Survey conducted in 2008 (target cohorts born from 1963 to 1980), Suga (2011) found no effect of educational attainment on the timing of resignation among women who were employed before marriage.

As seen from the foregoing information, previous findings suggest that change in the effect of educational attainment on women's employment in the child-rearing years, if any, occurred in cohorts born after the 1960s. Studies that examined data that included many women born before the 1960s found no effect of educational attainment on women's employment. However, a relatively large number of studies examining data on many women born after the 1960s (at this point, up to the 1980s cohort) found a positive effect of educational attainment on women's employment rate in the child-rearing years.

However, the change observed among the 1960s cohorts and onward might have occurred only during the 1990s. This is a possibility because many of the studies targeting women born after the 1960s that found a positive effect of educational attainment on their employment used data from surveys conducted in the 1990s. On the other hand, many studies targeting those born after the 1960s that used data from surveys conducted after 2000 found no such effect.

Husband's income

Women's decisions on whether to participate in the labour force are possibly influenced by their husbands' economic situations. Especially during the child-rearing years, the husbands' higher income could hinder women's employment.

Almost all studies that examined data on women born from the 1920s to the 1980s found a negative effect of husband's income on women's employment, regardless of employment status (e.g. regular, non-regular or self-employed) (Kojima, 1995; Nagase, 1994, 1999; Shintani, 1998). However, no effect of husband's income was found in study that controlled for the effect of the husband working in public office (a workplace that typically has regular hours and little overtime work) (Osawa and Suzuki, 2000). It shows that women whose husbands worked in public offices were more likely to work continuously as full-time employees after childbirth. It suggests that women's employment is influenced not only by their husbands' income, which affects their financial stability, but also by the husband's possible balance between work and family life.

Some studies not limited to women in their child-rearing years have found that husbands' higher income no longer hinders women's employment because the number of households in which both the husband and wife earn a high income has increased (Kohara, 2001; Ojima, 2011). However, findings from studies that focus on women's employment during the child-rearing years suggest that husbands' higher income still tends to hinder women's employment.

Parents' support

Sources of social support that assist women's employment are not limited to parents. The husband's support in household chores and child rearing, the help of older children in household chores, support from brothers, sisters and neighbourhood networks, and paid household and childcare support, such as babysitters, can also facilitate women's employment. However, many previous studies have almost exclusively examined parental support as a form of social support for women's employment during the child-rearing years. Moreover, these studies examined the effect of such support by looking at the residential relationship with parents. This partly reflected the child-rearing reality of the targeted cohorts (those born after about the 1940s). That is, although the proportion of three-generation households among households with children is gradually declining, 18% of households with children were still three-generation households in 2012 (calculated from published tables of the Basic Survey on People's Livelihood, by Ministry of Health, Labour and Welfare, Japan). It was thought that the intergenerational support relationship was more likely to emerge in three-generation households, and the effect of such a support relationship on women's employment was the focus of previous studies.

Indeed, many previous studies found a positive effect of three-generation households on women's employment. Kojima (1995) found that co-residing with either the wife's or the husband's parents increased the likelihood of women being continuously employed full-time during the infancy of their first child. Nagase (1999) found that co-residence with parents facilitated women's regular and non-regular employment after the birth of their first child. Using the same data (the 11th National Fertility Survey conducted in 1997), Shintani (1998) examined the effect of support from parents, not the distance of residence from parents, finding that support from parents enhanced the likelihood of women being employed (full-time, part-time or self-employed) during the first year after the birth of their first child. Furthermore, Yu (2009) examined data from the SSM and conducted a comparative analysis between Japan and Taiwan. She found that co-residence with parents prevented women's resignation before and after the first childbirth, and the size of the effect was larger in Japan than in Taiwan.

However, some studies suggest that the kind of co-residence with parents that had a positive effect on women's employment has varied by cohort (or generation). Senda (2002) showed that co-residence with either the wife's or the husband's mother at the time of the first birth had a positive effect on continuous regular employment of women born in 1958 or earlier, but only co-residence with the husband's mother had such an effect for women born in 1959 or later. On the other hand, Nishimura (2013) examined the effect of the distance of residence from the wife's and husband's mothers on women's employment, using the 1st, 2nd and 3rd National Family Research of Japan (NFRJ). The results showed no clear effect of these factors on women's employment in the 1998 and 2003 data. However, in the 2008 data, the distance of residence of the husband's mother had no effect on women's employment, but co-residence with the wife's mother had a positive effect on women being regular employees, and proximate residence to the wife's mother positively affected women's regular and non-regular employment.

Some studies on women born after the 1960s have found no effect of co-residence with parents or support from relatives on women's employment in the child-rearing years. Osawa and Suzuki (2000) reported that co-residence with parents did not have any effect on continuous full-time employment of women from 1 year before childbirth to the year of birth. Moreover, Imada and Ikeda (2006) reported that support from relatives coupled with use of childcare leave and day-care centres positively affected the employment of women born from the 1950s to the 1960s from 1 year before first childbirth to time of birth, while the use of childcare leave coupled with day-care centres (or also with support from relatives) positively affected the employment of women born from 1961 to 1975. They argued that sources of support that would facilitate women's continuous employment were changing from support from relatives to support from society. Whether the effect of support from relatives is waning, especially support from parents, needs to be further explored.

Data analysis on women born from the 1960s to the 1970s

Different aspects of the child-rearing period

This section presents a detailed analysis of women born from the 1960s to the 1970s. As discussed in Chapter 3, women born during this period experienced childbirth and child rearing in the late 1990s and early 2000s, when the Japanese economy was struggling. During this period, the number of non-regular employees was increasing in the labour market, and various social policies for supporting women's employment were being put forward while the birth rate was declining. This section examines factors hindering women's employment during this period.

For the analysis, data from the JPSC are used. The following section examines factors determining women's employment at various stages from childbirth and during the child-rearing years. Previous studies have targeted different phases of women's life courses when examining their employment. Some studies examined continuous employment of women from their first pregnancy to 1 year after childbirth, and others examined it during the first child's infancy or until the youngest child turned 6. Changes in women's employment during these various phases and differences in the factors determining women's employment status have not been explored.

Therefore, this section examines factors determining women's employment during various life-course phases. Specifically, it examines women's employment from 2 years before their first childbirth to the year of birth, at 1 year after their first birth and during the first decade after their first childbirth. Of course, these phases do not include all the various phases of the child-rearing years, but by making these distinctions (although these are limited to the first birth), we will be able to interpret how the factors determining women's employment function at various phases: before the birth of their first child, after the first birth and during the overall child-rearing period (considering, of course, that women can have additional pregnancies during the 10 years after the birth of their first child). In many previous studies, continuous employment from 1 year before childbirth has been examined; however, in this section, continuous employment from 2 years before childbirth is examined. This is because, as discussed in Chapter 4, most women born from the 1960s to the 1970s were in the labour force 2 years before childbirth, but the number fell drastically by 1 year before childbirth and by the year of birth. This means that by 1 year before childbirth, a good number of women have already left the labour force. It is therefore necessary to examine factors associated with continuous employment starting from 2 years before the birth of their first child until the year of birth.

The main factors examined here are women's human capital, household economic status and social support. In addition, to examine the effects of the labour market and social policies in detail, the indicator of labour supply and demand and year of first childbirth is examined.

The effect of women's human capital is measured by women's educational attainment (junior high or high school/junior, technical or vocational college/university or higher), type of occupation (professional or technical/clerical work/sales or service/manual labour/teaching),[1] firm size (1 to 99 employees/100 to 999 employees/over 1000 employees/public office) and their age at the birth of their first child, which is considered a proxy for years in the labour market. Household economic status is measured by husbands' annual income. As for social support, the possibility of support from parents and husbands is examined. The possibility of support from parents is measured by the distance of residence (co-residence/same town or within 1 km/others: within the same ward, municipality, prefecture, outside the prefecture, deceased parents)[2]; the possibility of support from the husband is measured by a dummy variable for whether the husband works in public offices. Although public offices can differ greatly, many of these workplaces seem generally accommodating to husbands who take care of their families. The year of the first birth is divided into three categories: the 1980s, 1990s and 2000s. The unemployment rate is used as a measurement of the state of supply and demand in the labour market.

Women's employment from 2 years before the first birth until the year of birth

Table 5.1 presents results of logistic regression analysis examining effects of women's educational attainment, year of first childbirth and unemployment rate on women's employment in the year of first birth for women who were employed 2 years before, and on regular employment in the year of first birth for women who were regular employees 2 years before. The results for the 1960s and 1970s cohorts are shown separately. Means and standard deviations of variables used in this analysis are shown in Appendix Table S.1.

The JPSC asks respondents retrospectively to report their employment status for each year after they turned 18. This allows for examination of pre- and post-pregnancy employment status of women who had given birth to their first child before the beginning of the survey. Analysis of a greater number of subjects is made possible using such retrospective data. In addition, such data allow for comparison between women who gave birth in the 1980s and those who did so in the 1990s and 2000s. However, analyses including information on the type of occupation and on their husbands or

Table 5.1 Logistic regression models predicting employment status at the year of the first childbirth

	Model 1								Model 2			
	1960s birth cohort				1970s birth cohort				1960s & 1970s birth cohorts			
	Employed → employed		Regular → regular		Employed → employed		Regular → regular		Employed → employed		Regular → regular	
	B	Exp(B)	B	Exp(B)	B	Exp(B)	B	Exp(B)	B	Exp(B)	B	Exp(B)
Constant	−1.234	—	−3.027	—	−0.486	—	−1.519	—	−10.877	—	−6.417	—
Educational attainment												
Junior high school or high school	—	—	—	—	—	—	—	—	—	—	—	—
Junior college	0.074	1.077	0.187	1.205	0.067	1.069	−0.102	0.903	0.662	1.938	−0.447	0.640
University	0.548†	1.173	1.236***	3.442	−0.052	0.949	0.140	1.150	−0.244	0.784	−0.960	0.383
Year of first birth												
1980s	−0.004	0.996	−0.011	0.989								
1990s	—	—	—	—	—	—	—	—				
2000s	0.182	1.200	−0.847	0.429	−0.126	0.882	−0.101	0.904				
Unemployment rate, 2 years before birth	0.199	1.220	0.767**	2.154	−0.024	0.976	0.222	1.249	−0.283	0.753	−0.281	0.755
Birth cohort												
1960s									—	—	—	—
1970s									0.724	2.063	1.751	5.760
Age at the first childbirth									0.281*	1.324	0.210	1.233

Regular employee at 2 years before birth	2.438***	11.451		
Firm size, 2 years before birth				
1–99	0.147	1.159	-1.139	0.320
100–999	0.225	1.252	-0.472	0.624
≥1000	—	—	—	—
Public sector	2.133*	8.443	3.867*	47.817
Occupation, 2 years before birth				
Professional			0.341	1.405
Clerical			—	—
Service and sales			-4.093	0.017
Manual labour			0.034	1.409
Teaching			0.467	1.596
Residence distance from parents				
Co-residence	0.657	1.928	1.648	5.197
Proximate residence	1.484	4.410	2.013	7.482
Parents lived further away than the same town, parents deceased	—	—	—	—

(Continued)

Table 5.1 (Continued)

	Model 1								Model 2			
	1960s birth cohort				1970s birth cohort				1960s & 1970s birth cohorts			
	Employed → employed		Regular → regular		Employed → employed		Regular → regular		Employed → employed		Regular → regular	
	B	Exp(B)	B	Exp(B)	B	Exp(B)	B	Exp(B)	B	Exp(B)	B	Exp(B)
Husband's income, 2 years before birth									−0.001	0.999	0.000	1.000
Husband's public-sector employment, 2 years before birth									0.461	1.585	−0.805	0.447
N	717		538		503		352		117		73	
Log likelihood	−459.470		−313.070		−323.903		−221.037		−51.634		−30.406	
LR χ^2	8.310		27.030		0.950		2.730		53.550		40.040	
Prob > χ^2	0.140		0.000		0.917		0.605		0.000		0.001	
Pseudo R^2	0.009		0.041		0.002		0.006		0.342		0.397	

Source: JPSC.

Note: Analyses were conducted for women who were either employed or regular employees at 2 years before the first childbirth.

$^\dagger p < .10$, $^* p < .05$, $^{**} p < .01$, $^{***} p < .001$.

parents are not possible since the information contained in retrospective data is limited.

Results from Model 1 of Table 5.1 on women born in the 1960s show that among those employed 2 years before their first birth, university graduates were more likely to remain in employment in the year of birth than their counterparts who graduated only from junior high or high school (although this is statistically significant at only the 10% level). The year of birth and the unemployment rate 2 years before the first birth did not have any significant effect on employment. Similarly, among those who were regular employees 2 years before the first birth, university graduates were significantly more likely to be in regular employment at the year of birth. The high unemployment rate 2 years before childbirth positively affects women's regular employment at their first birth.

As for women born in the 1970s, women's educational attainment, year of first childbirth and unemployment rate did not have a significant effect on employment or regular employment in the year of birth.

These results show the effect of university education on regular employment only among women born in the 1960s, whereas the effect was absent among those born in the 1970s. Similarly, the effect of the unemployment rate 2 years before the first childbirth positively affected the regular employment only of those born in the 1960s.

Why was the effect of educational attainment present only among women born in the 1960s?

The finding that higher educational attainment enhanced women's employment for those born in the 1960s, but not in the 1970s, can be explained as follows. The linkage between university education and regular employment (or stable employment with good benefits) was stronger in the 1960s birth cohort, and female university graduates born in the 1960s had greater opportunities of finding regular employment. However, the linkage became weaker for the 1970s birth cohort because the number of non-regular employees in the labour market increased. Moreover, women born in the 1960s who were able to find relatively good positions – that is, regular employment – were probably more likely to remain in those positions during a recession, in order to avoid various life risks, such as husband's wage erosion and job loss. Table 5.2 shows the relationship between educational attainment of women in the 1960s and 1970s birth cohorts and their employment status in the year of their first birth. Women in the 1960s birth cohort with university or higher education were more likely to be regular employees than those without such education; yet, this difference was not great among women in the 1970s birth cohort. This suggests that the linkage between university

Table 5.2 Distribution of employment status in the year of the first childbirth by birth cohort and educational attainment

	(%)					
	1960s birth cohort			*1970s birth cohort*		
	Junior high school or high school	*Junior college*	*University*	*Junior high school or high school*	*Junior college*	*University*
Regular	18.2	23.7	43.8	21.7	24.3	27.0
Non-regular	5.3	4.9	2.7	8.3	6.2	3.2
Self-employed	9.9	7.5	2.7	4.8	4.8	1.6
Not employed	66.7	64.0	50.7	65.2	64.8	68.3
Total	100	100	100	100	100	100

Source: JPSC.

education and regular employment in the year of the first birth was stronger for the 1960s cohort and weaker for the 1970s cohort. This is attributed to the change in relationship between educational attainment and regular employment (jobs with benefits that allow women to remain in the labour force), a change that occurred with the increasing number of non-regular employees in the labour market during the 1990s and early 2000s.

Effects of women's occupation, household economic status and social support on women's employment in the year of first birth

This section examines effects of women's occupation, household economic status and family support 2 years before childbirth on employment of women who gave birth after the survey began. Because the sample size is small, the analysis is conducted without dividing samples by birth cohort.

Model 2 in Table 5.1 examines the effects of women's occupation, age of their first child, husband's income and the possibility of support from the husband or parents 2 years before first childbirth on women's employment and regular employment in the year of first birth. For employment in the year of birth, the following variables' effects were considered: women's educational attainment, unemployment rate 2 years before the birth, birth cohort, age at the birth of the first child, whether the woman was a regular employee 2 years before the birth, the size of the firm at which the woman worked 2 years before the birth, distance of residence from parents, husband's income and whether the husband worked in public offices. When considering regular employment, in addition to these other variables, the effect of type of occupation 2 years before the birth was also considered.

Results show that age at the birth of the first child, regular employment 2 years before the birth and working in public offices (vs. working at a firm with over 1000 employees) positively affected women's employment in the year of birth. As for regular employment, those who worked in public offices were more likely to be regular employees in the year of the birth.

As mentioned, working in public offices and being a regular employee before birth were two significant factors that affected employment in the year of first birth. When only regular employment was considered, working in public offices showed the greatest effect on regular employment in the year of birth. In contrast, educational attainment showed no effect.

This suggests that for employment from 2 years before childbirth until the year of birth, the type of workplace (public office) and employment status (regular employee) are significantly important. Educational attainment may make it more likely for women to find positions as regular employees or in workplaces that will allow them to remain in the labour force, but it does not necessarily facilitate their employment per se.

These results also show that only women who are in specific workplaces or who hold a specific employment status are able to remain in the labour force until childbirth. Since only women who work in public offices or those who are regular employees are able to remain in the labour force, all other women employed at other workplaces or those who are not regular employees are not afforded the opportunity to remain in the labour force until childbirth. Therefore, as discussed in Chapter 4, as many as 70% of women born in the 1960s and 1970s were outside the labour force in the year of childbirth.

Women's employment 1 year after childbirth

This section examines factors determining women's employment and regular employment 1 year after their first childbirth. Factors considered are women's educational attainment, unemployment rate in the year of birth, birth cohort, age at the birth of the first child, distance of residence from parents in the year of birth, husband's annual income in the year of birth and whether the husband worked in public office in the year of the birth. In addition, women's first occupation[3] is considered.

Table 5.3 presents results from the analysis of factors associated with employment and regular employment of women 1 year after childbirth. Appendix Table S.2 shows means and standard deviations. The following factors positively affected employment: the 1970s birth cohort (vs. the 1960s cohort), age at the birth of the first child, being a professional worker or

Table 5.3 Logistic regression models predicting employment status at 1 year after the first childbirth and work continuation for 10 years after the first childbirth

	1 year after the first childbirth				10 years after the first childbirth			
	Employed vs. not employed		Regular vs. others		Continuous employment vs. others		Continuous regular employment vs. others	
	B	Exp(B)	B	Exp(B)	B	Exp(B)	B	Exp(B)
Constant	−3.221		−3.833		−1.827		−5.059	
Educational attainment								
Junior high school or high school	—		—		—		—	
Junior college	0.023	1.023	−0.495	0.610	−0.315	0.730	0.099	1.104
University	0.378	1.460	0.240	1.271	−0.299	0.742	0.304	1.356
Unemployment rate, at the year of birth	−0.132	0.876	−0.274	0.760	−0.308	0.735	−0.026	0.975
Birth cohort								
1960s	—		—					
1970s	0.736*	2.088	0.601	1.824				
Age at the first childbirth	0.081*	1.084	0.109*	1.115	0.047	1.048	0.069	1.072
First occupation								
Professional	1.155***	3.174	1.347***	3.845	0.816*	2.260	0.963*	2.619
Clerical	—		—		—		—	
Service and sales	−0.022	0.988	−0.450	0.638	−0.262	0.770	−1.237	0.290
Manual labour	0.628	1.873	0.107	1.113	0.279	1.322	0.654	1.923
Self-employed	0.656	1.927	0.483	1.621	2.144***	8.531	0.969	2.637
Teaching	1.121**	3.069	1.489**	4.431	1.201**	3.322	1.391**	4.020

Residence distance from parents								
Co-residence	0.671*	1.957	1.109***	3.030				
Proximate residence	0.493	1.638	0.331	1.393				
Parents lived further away than the same town, parents deceased	—	—	—	—				
Husband's income at the year of birth	−0.002*	0.998	−0.002	0.998				
Husband's public-sector employment at the year of birth	0.872***	2.391	1.059**	2.883				
Number of children at latest wave								
One					—	—	—	—
Two					−0.313	0.731	0.606	1.833
Three or more					−0.535	0.586	0.524	1.689
N	483		483		704		704	
Log likelihood	−250.426		−197.427		−291.049		−172.761	
LR χ²	57.720		63.710		31.490		35.550	
Prob > χ²	0.000		0.000		0.001		0.000	
Pseudo R²	0.103		0.139		0.051		0.093	

Source: JPSC.

Note: For models predicting employment status 1 year after the first childbirth samples were restricted to women who have children and whose husbands' and parents' related information at the year of the first childbirth is known. For models predicting work continuation for 10 years after the first childbirth samples were restricted to women whose eldest child is over 10 years old.

* p<.05, ** p<.01, *** p<.001

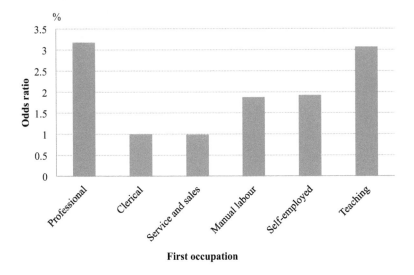

Figure 5.1 Occupational effects on women's employment 1 year after the first child-birth.

Source: JPSC.

Note: The odds ratios are shown in Table 5.3 of the model predicting employment status 1 year after the first childbirth for "employed vs. not employed." Other predictors in the model include educational attainment, unemployment rate for the year of the first childbirth, birth cohort, age at the first childbirth, residence distance from parents, husband's income and husband's public sector employment.

schoolteacher (vs. clerical worker), co-residence with parents, lower income of husband and husband's public sector employment. The following factors positively affected regular employment 1 year after childbirth: age at the birth of the first child, being a professional worker or schoolteacher (vs. clerical worker), co-residence with parents, lower income of husband and husband's public sector employment. Women's educational attainment did not have a significant effect on either employment or regular employment. Figures 5.1 and 5.2 show the effects of women's first occupation and residence distance from parents on women's employment 1 year after childbirth. Effects are presented as an odds ratio against clerical work (for Figure 5.1) and against those whose parents live further than in the same town (for Figure 5.2). The bars in Figure 5.1 indicate that women who had professional jobs or were schoolteachers were more likely to be employed 1 year after birth compared with those who had clerical jobs. The bars in Figure 5.2 show that those who lived with or close to parents were more likely to be employed compared to those whose parents lived further away than the same town.

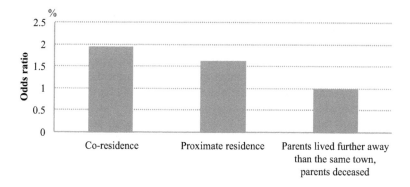

Figure 5.2 Effects of residence distance from parents on women's employment 1 year after the first childbirth.

Source: JPSC.

Note: The odds ratios are shown in Table 5.3 of the model predicting employment status 1 year after the first childbirth for "employed vs. not employed." Other predictors in the model include educational attainment, unemployment rate for the year of the first childbirth, birth cohort, age at the first childbirth, first occupation, husband's income and husband's public sector employment.

Although different variables were used, factors that influenced women's employment from 2 years before childbirth until the year of birth are quite similar to those influencing women's employment 1 year after childbirth. Although women's first occupation was not necessarily the same as their occupation before childbirth, professional workers or schoolteachers who continued to work at the same occupation until the year of birth were more likely to remain in the labour force 1 year after childbirth. Moreover, professional workers and schoolteachers were more likely to be employed 1 year after childbirth because these types of workplaces (e.g. schools and hospitals) are more likely to provide better working environments for working women with children.

Continuous employment during the decade immediately after childbirth

A further analysis was conducted to examine factors that influenced continuous employment or continuous regular employment during 10 years after the first childbirth of women who had given birth and whose first child was over 10 years old at the time of the survey. Husband's income, distance of residence from parents and husband's occupation were not considered since they could vary over time. Only women's educational attainment, unemployment rate in the year of birth, age at the birth of first child, type of first occupation and number of children at the time of the latest survey were considered. Table 5.3 (p. 58–9) shows the results. The type of first occupation had a significant effect; women who were professionals, self-employed workers or schoolteachers were more likely to remain in the labour force than those who were clerical workers. The type of first occupation also significantly affected continuous regular employment, and women who were professionals or schoolteachers were more likely to remain regular employees.

Summary: women's employment during the child-rearing years and the labour market and social policies in Japan

The effect of educational attainment on women's employment and regular employment from 2 years before childbirth until the year of birth was significant only in the 1960s cohort, not in the 1970s cohort. This was probably due to the increased number of non-regular employees in the labour market, beginning in the late 1990s, when many women born in the 1970s experienced life events, such as graduation, marriage and childbirth. Under these circumstances, many found it difficult to obtain stable jobs (regular employment with benefits) that would allow them to remain in the labour market. The difference in educational attainment's effect on women's employment between cohorts can be explained by the presence or absence of a linkage between university education and regular employment. Such linkage was present in the 1960s cohort, but not in the 1970s cohort.

Although educational attainment positively affected the 1960s cohort, it appears that higher educational attainment increased women's likelihood of finding jobs that would allow them to remain in the labour market (not that it facilitated women's employment per se). When employment status before childbirth and firm size where women worked were controlled, the effect of educational attainment disappeared. Women who were regular employees or who worked in public offices before childbirth were more likely to be employed and/or regular employees from before birth until the year of birth. In other words, among women born in the 1960s and 1970s, those who could remain in the labour market from before childbirth to after it were limited to public sector employees and/or regular employees.

Only women who could find workplaces or jobs that would allow them to remain in the labour market did so until childbirth, and this did not change even after the birth. The likelihood of women being employed (or in regular employment) in the first year after childbirth was higher among those whose first job was as a professional worker or schoolteacher than among those whose first job was as a clerical worker. The type of first occupation also affected women's continuous employment and continuous regular employment during the decade immediately after childbirth. Professional and teaching positions often require certain qualifications, so they tend to be stable employment. Only women employed at workplaces such as schools and hospitals that are conducive to family responsibilities can remain in the labour market during the child-rearing years. To put this another way, it is difficult for women who are not professional workers or schoolteachers to continue working after childbirth.

Analyses in this chapter also found that the domestic situation, such as the husband's income and the possibility of support from parents or the husband (whether the husband worked in public office, distance of residence from parents), was associated with women's employment.

It can be inferred that it remains difficult for women to stay in the labour market throughout their childbirth and child-rearing years, and this continuing difficulty was attributed to increasing numbers of non-regular employees in the labour market as well as to women's difficulties in building careers in the firm-specific internal labour market. For women to stay in the labour market during their childbirth and child-rearing years, it seems important that they become regular employees. This is because Japanese firms provide only regular employees with support during child-rearing years, pay raises and promotions commensurate with their length of service. However, because private firms expect their workers to prioritise work over family, women have difficulty continuing work as regular employees in private firms. Therefore, many women who remain in the labour market as regular employees are public sector employees or professional workers at schools or hospitals. However, women are now being given even fewer opportunities to become regular employees because the number of non-regular employees in the labour market has increased since the 1990s. Therefore, women's continuous employment during their child-rearing years remains difficult. Social policies supporting women's employment, such as childcare leave, began to be implemented from the 1990s to the 2000s. However, such policies cannot provide sufficient support to women who work at private firms with inflexible schedules, and few non-regular employees are able to use childcare leave.

Ironically, only those in regular employment can easily enjoy the benefits of social polices intended to encourage women's employment, while the number of young women in non-regular employment continues to grow. The 2004 amendment to the Childcare Leave Act grants even workers under fixed-term employment contracts the right to use childcare leave if they have been employed by the same employers for over 1 year, and they are expected to continue working after completion of the leave. In many cases, however, non-regular employees find it hard to obtain assurance from employers that their employment will continue after completion of the leave. As a consequence, the number of workers who can benefit from the system is still limited. Disparity between the treatment of regular and non-regular employees in the labour market thus emerges in the system of social policies. This, in turn, has created a gap in availability of social services among various employment statuses.

Notes

1 Teaching positions are often put into the category of professional or technical jobs in many studies. However, the JPSC has a separate category for teaching. In addition, examination of the effect of teaching positions on women's employment is an important one. Therefore, in this study, teaching is considered as an occupational category and its effects on women's employment are examined.
2 The parents who lived closer are considered in the analysis.
3 "Self-employed" is not an occupational category in exact sense. However, because it seems meaningful to investigate women's career development processes, it is used as an occupational category in the analyses which consider women's first occupation.

References

Imada, Sachiko. 1996. Joshi rōdō to shūgyō keizoku (Women's work and employment continuation). *The Japanese Journal of Labour Studies*, 433: 37–48.
Imada, Sachiko, & Shingo Ikeda. 2006. Shussan josei no koyō keizoku ni okeru ikuji kyūgyō seido no kōka to ryōritsu no kadai (The effect of childcare leave on women's work continuation after childbirth, and agenda on supporting work-family compatibility). *The Japanese Journal of Labour Studies*, 553: 34–44.
Kohara, Miki. 2001. Sengyō shufu ha yūfuku na katei no shōchō ka (Is the full-time housewife a symbol of a wealthy family?). *The Japanese Journal of Labour Studies*, 493: 15–29.
Kojima, Hiroshi. 1995. Kekkon, shussan, ikuji oyobi shūgyō (Marriage, childbirth, childrearing, and employment). In Hiroshi Obuchi (Ed.), *Josei no raifu saikuru to shūgyō kōdō* (Women's life cycle and employment behaviour) (pp. 61–87). Tokyo: Printing Bureau, Ministry of Finance of Japan.
Ministry of Health, Labour and Welfare, Japan. Various years. *Kokumin seikatsu kiso chōsa* (Basic Survey on People's Livelihood). Retrieved from http://www.mhlw.go.jp/toukei/list/20–21kekka.html (accessed March 24, 2014).
Nagase, Nobuko. 1994. Kikon joshi no koyō shūgyō keitai no sentaku ni kansuru jisshō bunseki (Empirical analysis on employment status choice among married women). *The Japanese Journal of Labour Studies*, 418: 31–42.

Nagase, Nobuko. 1999. Shōshika no yōin: shūgyō kankyō ka kachikan no henka ka (Factors of declining fertility: employment circumstances or change of values?). *Journal of Population Problems*, 55(2): 1–18.

Nishimura, Junko. 2013. *What determines employment of Japanese women with infants?: Comparison among National Family Research of Japan (NFRJ) 1998, 2003, and 2008*. Paper presented at International Sociological Association Research Committee Spring Conference, Taipei.

Ojima, Fumiaki. 2011. Tsuma no shūgyō to shotoku kakusa (Wives' employment and income disparity). In Yoshimichi Sato & Fumiaki Ojima (Eds.), *Gendai no kaisō shakai 1* (The contemporary stratification society, 1) (pp. 113–127). Tokyo: University of Tokyo Press.

Osawa, Machiko. 1993. *Keizai henka to joshi rōdō: nichibei no hikaku kenkyū* (Economic change and women's employment: Comparison between Japan and the US). Tokyo: Nihon Keizai Hyoronsha.

Osawa, Machiko, & Haruko Suzuki. 2000. Josei no kekkon, shussan oyobi jinteki shihon keisei ni kansuru paneru dēta bunseki (Panel data analysis on women's marriage, childbirth, and formation of human capital). *Japanese Journal of Research on Household Economics*, 48: 45–53.

Senda, Yukiko. 2002. Kikon josei no shūgyō keizoku to ikuji shigen no kankei (The association between married women's work continuation and childcare resources). *Journal of Population Problems*, 58(2): 2–21.

Shintani, Yuriko. 1998. Kekkon, shussanki no josei no shūgyō to sono kitei yōin (Women's employment in marriage and childbirth stage and their determinants). *Journal of Population Problems*, 54(4): 46–62.

Suga, Keita. 2011. Yūhaigū joshi no wāku raifu baransu to raifu kōsu (Work life balance and life course among married women). *Journal of Population Problems*, 67(1): 1–23.

Tanaka, Shigeto. 1998. Kōgakurekika to seibetsu bungyō (Popularisation of higher education and division of labour). In Kazuo Seiyama & Sachiko Imada (Eds.), *1995 nen SSM chōsa shirīzu 12: Josei no kyaria kōzō to sono henka* (Research series of 1995 SSM survey No. 12: Structure of women's career and its change) (pp. 1–16). Tokyo: Research association for 1995 SSM survey.

Yu, Wei-hsin. 2009. *Gendered trajectories: Women, work, and social change in Japan and Taiwan*. Stanford: Stanford University Press.

6 Re-entry and exit again?

Women's careers after childbirth through the post-child-rearing years

Women's employment after the birth of the first child

Post-child-rearing years and women's employment

This chapter will explore Japanese women's employment and their careers for the period from birth of their first child to the post-child-rearing years (defined as the period beginning when the youngest child enters school and ending when the youngest child graduates from high school). In this chapter, the post-child-rearing years refers to the parent's life stage when children no longer require extremely time-intensive care, but still require some parental care and some attention to their education. Although many studies have been conducted on women's employment during their child-rearing years, not much attention has been paid to women's employment during their post-child-rearing years and the factors affecting it. While many women leave their jobs for marriage and childbirth as discussed in previous chapters, many of these women re-enter the labour force during their post-child-rearing years. As Nishimura (2009) points out, it is during these post-child-rearing years that many women confront the issue of how to balance work and family.

However, little has been uncovered regarding women's employment and their careers during their post-child-rearing years. This is probably related to the fact that many women at this life stage engage in non-regular employment, such as part-time jobs. Since most of non-regular work is part-time with fewer responsibilities, it has been believed that it is easy for non-regular employees to balance work and family. Nevertheless, non-regular employees, such as part-time workers, are not a homogeneous group, as seen in the debate for the mobilisation of the part-timer workforce (Honda, 2010). Who these women who work outside the home during their post-child-rearing years are, what ways of working they engage in, and what factors affect their re-entrance to the labour market and subsequent career-building are questions that need answering.

Employment status after the birth of the first child

As in the previous chapters, the data from the JPSC will be used to describe women's employment status after the birth of the first child. Table 6.1 shows women's employment status by their first child's age for the 1960s and 1970s cohort. Because all available cases were included in each age column of their first child's age, the number of case varies across the age columns. Moreover, due to the research design of this survey, the number of cases decrease with the increase in age of the first child. The survey waves began when these women were in their mid- to late twenties (early thirties for women born in the 1960s). The data on the women's employment status when their first child's age was older were obtained from only those who remained in the survey for several waves. Therefore, fewer cases were available for analysis when women's first child was older than when the child was younger. In addition, since the respondents were asked to recall their past employment status retrospectively, those who had already had their first children when the survey waves began were able to give information on their employment status between the period after the birth of the first child and the beginning of the survey waves. This also contributed to the fact that the number of cases is somewhat higher in the left-hand columns. Fewer cases were available for the 1970s cohort than for the 1960s cohort because in many cases the first child of the women in the 1970s cohort had not reached the specified age by 2008.

Table 6.1 shows that around 70% of both cohorts were without a job when their first child was below 1 year of age. However, the percentage of those who were not employed decreased as their first child aged. When their first child was 12, women who were not employed decreased to about 35% for both cohorts. On the other hand, women who were engaged in non-regular employment increased as their first child aged. While the percentage of those who were engaged in non-regular employment when their first child was below 1 year of age was less than 10% for both cohorts, it increased to 37.4% and 41.9% when their first child was 12 for the 1960s cohort and the 1970s cohort, respectively. The percentage of women who were engaged in regular employment did not increase as their first child aged. This accounted for less than 20% of women for the entire time between when their first child was below 1 year of age and when he or she turned 12.

When differences between cohorts are examined more closely, several things become clear. First, the percentage of women who were not employed when their first child was young (between 1 and 5) was lower and that of those who were engaged in non-regular employment was higher for the 1970s cohort than the 1960s cohort. For example, 58.9% of the 1960s cohort was not employed when their first child was 5, but only 49.8% of the

Table 6.1 Distribution of women's employment status by their first child's age for the 1960s and 1970s birth cohorts

1960s birth cohort	(%)								
	Age 0	Age 1	Age 2	Age 3	Age 5	Age 7	Age 12	Age 15	Age 18
Regular	19.2	15.7	14.4	14.0	15.5	15.6	16.3	18.9	21.4
Non-regular	5.0	7.1	10.1	12.6	16.3	22.4	37.4	39.3	39.9
Self-employed	6.2	6.2	6.5	8.0	9.3	10.7	10.8	12.2	10.5
Not employed	69.6	71.1	69.0	65.4	58.9	51.4	35.5	29.6	28.1
Total	100	100	100	100	100	100	100	100	100
N	886	893	890	888	870	823	657	507	313

1970s birth cohort	Age 0	Age 1	Age 2	Age 3	Age 5	Age 7	Age 12		
Regular	19.8	16.0	14.6	14.0	14.6	12.7	16.2		
Non-regular	7.3	12.1	15.0	18.0	27.1	31.2	41.9		
Self-employed	3.9	4.2	5.8	8.0	8.6	7.6	5.7		
Not employed	69.1	67.8	64.6	50.0	49.8	48.5	36.2		
Total	100	100	100	100	100	100	100		
N	647	614	582	528	440	330	105		

Source: JPSC.

Note: Ages represent those of the first child.

1970s cohort was not. However, while only 16.3% of the 1960s cohort was engaged in non-regular employment when their first child was 5, this was as high as 27.1% in the 1970s cohort. Second, a higher percentage of the 1970s cohort were engaged in non-regular employment than the 1960s cohort, and a lower percentage of the 1970s cohort were self-employed than the 1960s cohort, regardless of the age of their first child.

What becomes clear from these observations is that many of the women who were not working at the time of birth of the first child re-entered the labour market by the time their first child graduated from elementary school, and many of those women who re-entered the labour market were engaged in non-regular employment. In addition, these observations suggest that women in different cohorts re-entered the labour market at different times relative to their first child's age. In other words, women of the 1970s birth cohort re-entered the labour market earlier than their 1960s counterparts, meaning that they were more likely to re-enter the labour market while their first child was still very young.

Change in employment status after the birth of the first child

Table 6.2 shows the changes in employment status of the women for both cohorts in each year during the first 10 years after the birth of the first child. Changes in employment status were categorized into the following five groups: continued employment with no change in status (continued regular employment, continued non-regular employment, continued self-employment), continued employment with a change in status (non-regular to regular employment, regular to self-employment, etc.), getting employed, resignation, and continued as being not employed.

Table 6.2 shows that approximately 10%–15% of women in both the 1960s and 1970s cohorts were continuously engaged in regular employment during the first 10 years after the birth of their first child. The percentage of women who were continuously engaged in non-regular employment increased over years, and the percentage reached over 20% for both 1960s and 1970s cohorts by the ninth year after the birth of the first child. However, the manner of increase differed between the cohorts. That is to say, an increase in continuous non-regular employment began to occur earlier after the birth of the first child for the 1970s cohort than the 1960s cohort, and about 20% of the 1970s cohort was continuously engaged in non-regular employment by the fourth and fifth year after the birth of the first child. In any given year, less than 10% of women were continuously self-employed, although the percentage was slightly higher for the 1960s cohort than their 1970s counterparts. The percentage of women who continued their employment after a change in status was not large, but for the 1970s cohort, the percentage increased gradually after the birth of the first child. More specifically, while the percentage was 1.5% during the first year after the birth of the first child, it increased to 6.4% during the ninth and tenth year. A higher percentage of the 1970s cohort re-entered the labour market in any given year after the birth of the first child than did the 1960s cohort. The peak in the percentage of those who re-entered the labour market occurred between the fifth and tenth year after the birth of the first child for the 1960s cohort, while it occurred a little earlier, between the third and fourth year after the birth of the first child for the 1970s cohort (at least the first peak). Only a small percentage of the respondents resigned from their jobs, and not much change in the percentage was observed during the 10 years. Only about 5% of the 1960s and 1970s cohorts resigned their jobs in each year. The percentage of those who were continuously not employed decreased as time went by after the birth of the first child. Over 60% of the 1960s and 1970s cohorts were not employed in the first year after the birth of the first child. However, the percentage decreased to around 35% during the ninth and tenth year after the birth of the first child.

Table 6.2 Changes in women's employment status in each year during the first 10 years after the birth of the first child for the 1960s and 1970s birth cohorts

1960s birth cohort	(%)									
	0–1 year	1–2 years	2–3 years	3–4 years	4–5 years	5–6 years	6–7 years	7–8 years	8–9 years	9–10 years
Continued regular employment	14.7	13.8	12.9	12.9	13.3	14.5	13.8	13.4	12.6	13.3
Continued non-regular employment	3.0	5.9	7.1	9.4	10.6	13.4	15.9	18.6	21.9	24.1
Continued self-employment	5.1	5.0	4.9	6.4	6.5	7.2	8.6	8.7	8.6	9.2
Continued employment with a change in status	1.3	1.4	1.8	1.8	2.3	2.0	2.3	3.4	4.2	3.7
Getting employed	4.3	4.9	7.5	6.6	8.3	8.1	7.8	7.9	9.5	8.2
Resignation	6.2	2.5	4.2	3.7	4.6	4.3	4.7	4.4	4.4	6.1
Continued as being not employed	65.4	66.5	61.5	59.2	54.4	50.4	46.9	43.7	38.9	35.5
Total	100	100	100	100	100	100	100	100	100	100
N	875	877	875	869	858	835	811	801	769	736

1970s birth cohort	(%)									
	0–1 year	1–2 years	2–3 years	3–4 years	4–5 years	5–6 years	6–7 years	7–8 years	8–9 years	9–10 years
Continued regular employment	14.2	13.7	11.2	11.9	11.9	11.3	10.0	11.6	13.4	12.9
Continued non-regular employment	5.1	8.4	10.4	14.9	19.4	21.7	25.5	23.3	23.0	25.7
Continued self-employment	3.0	4.0	5.3	6.6	5.7	5.9	5.8	5.5	4.8	4.7
Continued employment with a change in status	1.5	1.1	2.5	2.8	4.6	4.6	4.2	6.6	7.2	6.4
Getting employed	8.3	7.7	10.4	12.1	8.5	9.0	6.1	11.6	5.3	11.7
Resignation	6.4	4.6	5.9	4.7	5.0	5.6	6.4	5.8	11.5	4.1
Continued as being not employed	61.6	60.5	54.3	47.1	45.0	41.9	42.1	35.6	34.9	34.5
Total	100	100	100	100	100	100	100	100	100	100
N	606	569	527	471	438	391	330	275	209	171

Source: JPSC.

Note: Years represent time after the first childbirth.

These trends allow a clearer analysis of women's re-entrance to the labour market after the birth of the first child. In some years after the birth of the first child, as much as 10% of women re-entered the labour market. More and more women were continuously engaged in non-regular employment after the birth of the first child, while the percentage of those who were continuously engaged in regular employment did not change much. These findings in turn suggest that many of those women who re-entered the labour market did so as non-regular employees. Moreover, the peak in the percentage of women who re-entered the labour market occurred in the fifth year or later after the birth of the first child for the 1960s cohort, whereas it occurred around the third year after the birth of the first child for the 1970s cohort; that is, the 1970s cohort re-entered the labour market sooner than their 1960s counterparts. Furthermore, the fact that a certain number of women resigned and changed their employment status each year during the 10 years after the birth of the first child suggests that women were likely to experience change in their employment status after the birth of the first child.

As just described, many women enter (or, as is probable, re-enter) the labour market after the birth of the first child through their post-child-rearing years. Some experience changes in their employment status, and others resign. Who are these women who experience changes, and do they experience this change only once? What career paths do these women who have re-entered the labour market take? The next section will discuss these questions.

What determines women's re-entrance to the labour market?

Trends of re-entry

This section will explore the trends in women's re-entrance to the labour market from the JPSC using an event history analysis, which allows an analysis of the occurrence of a given event and its timing. Subjects of the analysis are women who were born in the 1960s or 1970s and who were not employed at the birth of the first child. Among them, those who had already re-entered the labour force at the time when the survey waves began (N = 272) were excluded, since some information at the time of the event, such as regarding their family situation, was missing. As a result, 911 women were included in the analysis.

Among the 911 women, 507 (55.6%) re-entered the labour market for the first time after the birth of the first child during the observation period. This number is about the same as seen in Hirao (2005) (data from those born between 1946 and 1965) and Sakamoto (2009) (JPSC data gathered in and before 2002). This suggests that the re-entrance rate of women born in the 1960s and 1970s, or slightly earlier, is around 60%.

However, this 60% is the number obtained without considering the time after the birth of the first child, birth year or various other characteristics. When and what groups of people re-enter the labour market and the likelihood that they do so remain unclear. Therefore, using Kaplan-Meier estimators, the percentage of those who re-enter the labour market over time for each cohort will be estimated. Since the previous section suggests that the 1970s cohort re-entered the labour market earlier than the 1960s cohort, the trend for each cohort will be examined separately.

Figure 6.1 shows the results of Kaplan-Meier estimates of the rate of women who re-entered the labour market after the birth of the first child for each cohort. The x-axis shows time after the birth of the first child in years, and the y-axis shows the survival rate of those who stay outside the labour market. Figure 6.1 shows that the percentage of those who remain outside the labour market in each year is over 80% until 5 years after the birth of the first child for both the 1960s and 1970s cohorts. After that point, the percentage decreases over time, but it does so faster for the 1970s cohort than the 1960s cohort. The percentage decreases to about 50% for the 1960s cohort and to 40% for the 1970s cohort at 10 years after the birth of the first

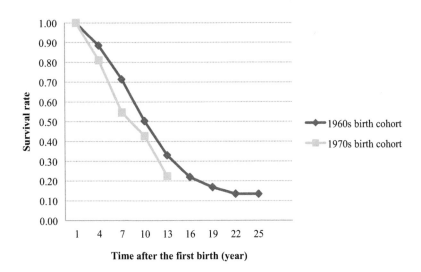

Figure 6.1 Survivor function for women's labour force entry after the first childbirth for the 1960s and the 1970s birth cohorts.

Source: JPSC.

child. By the fifteenth year after the birth of the first child, it decreases to 25% for the 1960s cohort and to around 20% for the 1970s cohort. To summarize, women outside the labour market at the birth of the first child begin to re-enter the labour market in the fifth year after the birth of the first child, and the probability that they remain outside the labour market is around 40%–50% and 20%–25% in the tenth and fifteenth year after the birth of the first child, respectively. In addition, the probability that they re-enter the labour market while their first child is still very young is higher for the 1970s cohort than the 1960s cohort.

Previous findings on determining factors for women's re-entrance to the labour market

Next, attention will be paid to several factors that are possibly related to women's re-entrance to the labour market. As in Chapter 5, three factors that previous research has argued impacts on women's employment will be reviewed. These factors are women's educational attainment, husbands' income and parents' support.

Not much research has been done on the type of women who re-enter the labour market after the birth of the first child. The limited number of studies include one by Hirao (2005) that used survey data collected through elementary schools in Nagoya from women born between 1946 and 1965; one by Yamato (2011) in which the data of 2005 was used to analyse whether women who were not employed at the birth of the youngest child re-entered the labour force; one by Sakamoto (2009) that used the JPSC data, as in this study, and examined the determining factors of the re-entrance to the labour market of women who were not employed in the year of the birth of the first child (data were limited to those from 2002 or earlier); a similar study by Higuchi (2007) (data were limited to those from 2006 or earlier); and a second study by Higuchi (2000) in which he, using the JPSC data, analysed the probability that women who were not employed in the previous year would enter the labour force (data were limited to those from 1998 or earlier). Some of these studies did not analyse women's re-entrance to the labour market, and they varied in that some began analysis at respondents' birth of the first child and others did so at the birth of the youngest child. Ahead are similarities and differences in the findings from these studies, with the understanding that they did not necessarily analyse the occurrence of the same event.

Hirao (2005), Higuchi (2000, 2007) and Sakamoto (2009) reported that women who graduate from university or higher are less likely to re-enter the labour market. However, when husbands' income is controlled for, the effect of women's educational attainment disappears in the studies by Hirao (2005) and Higuchi (2007), and the coefficient becomes smaller in the study by Sakamoto (2009). Conversely, Yamato (2011) argued that women's educational attainment has no effect on their re-entrance to the labour market as regular and non-regular employees, but that the educational attainment of a junior college degree or more has a positive effect on their re-entrance to the labour force as self-employed workers.

As shown, the effect of women's educational attainment on their re-entrance to the labour market has not clearly been confirmed. Women with a university education or higher may be less likely to re-enter the labour market, but the effect of women's educational attainment is quite small, as it disappears when husbands' income is controlled.

As for husbands' income, all the studies that examine its effect report that husbands' income has a statistically significant negative effect on women's re-entrance to the labour market (Higuchi, 2000, 2007; Hirao, 2005; Sakamoto, 2009). Moreover, Higuchi (2000) shows that a temporal decrease in the husband's income (change from the previous year) does not affect the wife's new employment, but a constant decrease in the husband's income (3 years moving average) positively affects the wife's new employment.

The effect of parents' support on women's re-entrance to the labour market is often measured by residence distance from a parent, but this is inconclusive. Hirao (2005) reports that women's co-residence with their husband's parents or their own parents does not have a statistically significant positive effect on women's re-entrance to the labour market. On the contrary, Sakamoto (2009) reports that residence distance from their husband's parents or their own parents has a negative effect on women's re-entrance to the labour market. This inconsistency may be due to the difference in the targeted cohorts of these studies. There was about a 10-year gap in the cohorts' age in these two studies. Hirao's study's targeted cohorts were born between 1946 and 1965, while Sakamoto's study included cohorts born between 1959 and 1973, or locality-specific variations (Hirao's study used data from Nagoya, whereas Sakamoto used the JPSC data collected from across the nation). Either way, what is important to note here is that the findings have been inconclusive.

Analysis of labour force re-entry

With these findings in mind, women's re-entrance to the labour market for the 1960s and 1970s cohorts from the JPSC data will be examined applying discrete-time logit models. The event in focus is women's first re-entrance to the labour force after the birth of the first child. Only those who had not re-entered the labour market for the first time after the birth of the first child at the time when the survey waves began will be included in the analysis. Factors that will be examined are basically similar to those discussed in Chapter 5. These are human capital factors, such as women's educational attainment, their first occupation and their age at the birth of the first child, which is a proxy of their years of experience in the labour market. Their husband's income will be used to measure their household's economic situation. As for social support, their residence distance from their husband's parents or their own parents and whether their husband works in public office are considered. Moreover, unemployment rate, which reflects the labour market's supply-demand conditions, and the number of children and the age of their youngest child, both of which may influence the timing of the women's re-entrance to the labour market, will be included in the analysis.

Table 6.3 shows the results of a discrete-time event history models on women's first re-entry to the labour market after the birth of the first child. Means and standard deviations of variables used in this analysis are shown in Appendix Table S.3. Time shows a significant effect that women are more likely to re-enter the labour market from a few years after their first childbirth to the time when their first child is in school age, compared with the first year after childbirth. Those who worked as a professional or were self-employed were more likely to re-enter the labour force than those who worked as a clerical worker for their first job. Women who resided with their husband's parents or their own parents and those who lived close to the parents were more likely to re-enter the labour market than those who resided far from the parents. Moreover, it shows that the women were less likely to re-enter the labour market when the husband's income was high and those whose youngest child were older were more likely to do so than those whose youngest child was still young.

Women's educational attainment as part of human capital did not have any effect on their re-entrance to the labour market. The women's first occupation, but not their educational attainment, had an effect on their re-entrance to the labour market. This is probably due to training systems for white-collar workers in the Japanese firm-specific internal labour market and the status of female clerical workers in a gendered work environment. That is to say, firms assume long-term employment of male clerks, and expect them to obtain firm-specific skills through on-the-job training, while they assign duties that do not require such training to female clerks under the assumption that they will resign at childbirth. Therefore, in many firms, positions probably do not exist for women who worked as clerks to return after birth and child rearing. These days, media sometimes feature companies that have a system for re-employing women who resigned for childbirth and child rearing. However, such a tendency has been limited to a group of mostly major firms, and their efforts have not been sufficient

Table 6.3 Discrete-time event history models predicting labour force re-entry after the first childbirth

	Coef.	*Exp(B)*
Time		
The year of birth to 1 year since birth	–	–
2–3 years since birth	1.103***	3.013
4–5 years since birth	1.164***	3.203
6–9 years since birth	1.279***	3.512
10–14 years since birth	1.123*	3.074
15 years or over since birth	−0.234	0.792
Educational attainment		
Junior high school or high school	–	–
Junior college	−0.110	0.856
University	−0.165	0.848
Unemployment rate	0.121	1.128
Birth cohort		
1960s	–	–
1970s	0.164	1.179
Age at the first birth	−0.021	0.980
First occupation		
Professional	0.395*	1.484
Clerical	–	–
Service and sales	−0.102	0.903
Manual labour	0.004	1.004
Self-employed	1.167*	3.212
Teaching	0.206	1.229
Residence distance from parents		
Co-residence	0.268*	1.307
Proximate residence	0.338*	1.402
Parents lived further away than the same town, parents deceased	–	–
Husband's income	−0.001***	0.999
Husband's public-sector employment	−0.156	0.855
Number of children	−0.041	0.960
Age of youngest child	0.142***	1.152
Constant	−3.218	
Log likelihood	−1303.321	
Person-year spells, n	4819	
LR χ^2 (d.f.)	174.24 (21)	
Prob > χ^2	0.000	

Source: JPSC.

Note: Analysis was conducted for women who were out of the labour force at the year of the first childbirth.

*$p < .05$, **$p < .01$,***$p < .001$.

to increase women's re-entrance to the labour market. Conversely, women who worked as a professional or self-employed worker are more likely to re-enter the labour market after childbirth, probably because they are able to build their career by alternate means than through the personnel training process at private firms. For example, their employment is based on their qualifications, or they re-enter the labour market to address a need of a family business, or they start their own business.

The results also imply that women's re-entrance to the labour market is difficult to realise without resources to support child rearing. The presence of women's husbands' parents or their own parents to act as resources to support household chores and child rearing seems to have played a significant role in when women decided to re-enter the labour force. When the effects of human capital and social support were controlled for, the effect of birth cohort disappeared.

What happens after women's re-entrance to the labour market

Destination of labour market re-entry: unknown areas

What career paths will women who have re-entered the labour market take? This aspect of the study of women's employment has long been ignored. The focus of studies on women's work career after the birth of a child generally focused exclusively on whether the women who were out of the labour force when they gave birth would re-enter the labour force. Needless to say, however, women's work career does not end simply when they re-enter the labour market. There are many questions still to be answered, such as what kinds of women take what kinds of career paths, and what factors hinder or facilitate their career-building. In fact, as discussed in an earlier section of this chapter, in each year of the 10 years after the birth of the first child, a certain number of women left their jobs or experienced changes in their employment status. This suggests the possibility that women who re-enter the labour market after the birth of a child can experience further changes in their employment status. This section will examine such changes experienced by women who re-entered the labour market after the birth of the first child. It will also clarify the factors that explain them.

Employment status at the time of re-entry and subsequent changes

As shown in previous section of this chapter, among 507 women who re-entered the labour market after the survey was begun, 23 (4.5%) of them returned as regular employees, while 378 (74.6%), and 106 (20.9%) of them did so as non-regular employees and self-employed workers, respectively. It is clear that an overwhelming majority of women re-entered the labour market as non-regular employees. This section will focus on what happened to these non-regular employees.

Out of 378 women who re-entered the labour force as non-regular employees, 205 (54.2%) of them experienced changes in their employment status during the survey period. Of these 205, 71 of them became regular employees or self-employed workers, and 134 of them exited the labour force again. This means that half of the women who re-entered the labour market as non-regular employees subsequently experienced some kind of change in their employment status and many of these changes were from being employed to being out of the labour force. This suggests a difficulty these women faced in building a career after re-entering the labour market.

Next, using Kaplan-Meier estimators, the percentage of women who experience changes in their employment status will be examined to find when they experience such changes. After re-entering the labour market, 45% of them remain as non-regular employees in the fifth year and 25.5% of them do so in the tenth year (figure not shown). This result shows that many of them experience changes in their employment status fairly early on.

Determinants for further changes in employment status after re-entry

The likelihood to experience changes in employment status after re-entry is examined applying multinomial logit models. A distinction is made between a shift from non-regular employment to regular or self-employment and a shift from non-regular employment to out of labour force. Factors to be considered include the women's educational attainment as human capital, their occupation when they re-entered the labour market as non-regular employees, age at the birth of the first child, their husband's income as an indicator of their household economic condition, their residence distance from their husband's parents or their own parents as a source of social support, whether their husband worked in public office, the number of children as a proxy of the burden of child rearing, the age of the youngest child, unemployment rate as a reflection of supply and demand in the labour market, and birth cohort.

Table 6.4 shows the results from a multinomial logit analysis. In contrast to those who did not experience any changes in their employment status as non-regular employees, factors determining the shift to regular employment or self-employment and those determining the exit from the labour market were examined. Means and standard deviations of variables used in this analysis are shown in Appendix Table S.4. Women's educational attainment, the age at the birth of the first child, their residence distance from their

Table 6.4 Multinomial logit models predicting changes in employment status after re-entry as non-regular employee

(Ref. continued non-regular employment)	Non-regular → Regular or self employed		Non-regular → Out of labour force	
	B	Exp(B)	B	Exp(B)
Constant	−2.297		−2.349	
Birth cohort				
1960s	−	−	−	−
1970s	0.598†	1.818	0.045	1.046
Occupation at re-entry				
Professional	0.168	1.183	−0.066	0.936
Clerical	−	−	−	−
Service and sales	−0.844*	0.430	0.294	1.342
Manual labour	−0.629	0.533	0.237	1.267
Teaching	−1.358	0.257	0.141	1.152
Husband's income	−0.002*	0.998	0.001†	1.000
Age of youngest child	0.037	1.038	−0.084 **	0.919
N	1450			
Log likelihood	−633.798			
LR χ^2	32.430			
Prob > χ^2	0.004			
Pseudo R^2	0.025			

Source: JPSC.

Note: Analysis was conducted for women who re-entered the labour force as non-regular employees after the first childbirth.

†$p < .10$, *$p < .05$, **$p < .01$,***$p < .001$.

husband's parents or their own parents, whether their husband worked in public office, the number of children and unemployment rate did not have any significant effect on the outcomes. Moreover, the model with all these factors itself was not significant, either. Therefore, Table 6.4 shows only the results from the model that included only birth cohort, occupation when they re-entered the labour market as non-regular employees, their husband's income and the age of their youngest child.

When we focus on the shift to regular or self-employment, we can see that those who were service or sales workers were less likely to experience such change in their employment status compared to those who were clerical workers. Higher husband's income negatively affects the likelihood to experience a shift to regular or self-employment. Those who were born in the 1970s are more likely to experience a shift to regular or self-employment, although it is significant only at the 10% level.

A shift to regular or self-employment can be considered positive for career development due to an expected increase in income, and discretion and responsibilities given at work. However, that shift was associated with the type of occupation the women held when they re-entered the labour force. Indeed, a large percentage of the women who re-entered the labour force did so as either a service worker (43.4%) or a manual worker (21.8%), and both of these occupations had a negative effect on the likelihood of the shift to regular or self-employment. This suggests that the route that would allow women to develop their careers as regular employees or self-employed workers was highly limited to the women who re-entered the labour market as non-regular employees. Yet, the greater likelihood of experiencing change to regular or self-employment among the 1970s birth cohort compared to the 1960s cohort could be due to recent corporate efforts to convert non-regular employees to regular employees.

When we turn to the labour force exit after re-entry as non-regular employees, the age of the women's youngest child and the husband's income significantly related to the women's likelihood to exit the labour force, although the husband's income was statistically significant at only the 10% level. It is likely that women who re-entered the labour market shortly after the birth of the first child found it difficult to work as well as manage household chores and child rearing, and had no other choice but to exit the labour market. Moreover, having a second or third child might have required them to dedicate themselves to child rearing again. If the husband's income was high, it is easy to imagine that women were more likely to exit from the labour force to avoid too much burden from work and family. Even after re-entering the labour market as non-regular employees, women were again confronted with the choice between child rearing and work.

What happens for women who were employed at the first childbirth

In this section, the subsequent career of women who held jobs at the birth of the first child will be examined. In Chapter 5 and the previous section of this chapter, we found that only a minority of women were employed at the birth of the first child and they were more likely to be professionals or regular employees at public offices. Factors that lead to these women exiting the labour market will be examined.

Kaplan-Meier survival curves were created to assess the survival rate (remain in the labour market) of women born in the 1960s and 1970s who were in the labour market at the birth of the first child (N = 410). The results show that the survival rate in the fifth, tenth and fifteenth year is 87.6%, 77.0% and 69.2%, respectively (figure not shown). The survival rate in the tenth year is over 75%, probably because they are generally fortunate in having an occupation and family background that allow them to remain in the labour market. Not many people nowadays are so fortunate, but the results show that when women have favourable conditions that allow them to remain in the labour market in the year of the birth of the first child, they are highly likely to remain in the labour market thereafter.

What factors contribute to women's exit from the labour force? Next, the effect of several factors on the likelihood of women's exit from the labour force will be examined, applying a discrete-time logit model. These factors include women's educational attainment, unemployment rate, birth cohort, age at the birth of the first child, their first occupation, their residence distance from their husband's parents or their own parents, their husband's income, their husband's public sector employment, the number of children and the age of their youngest child.

Table 6.5 shows the results from discrete-time logit model on exit from the labour force of women who were in the labour force at the birth of the first child. Appendix Table S.5 shows means and standard deviations. Compared to the women who started their career as clerical workers, those who were schoolteachers were less likely to exit the labour market, although it is significant at only the 10% level. In addition, compared to those who lived far from their husband's parents or their own parents, those who co-resided with their parents were less likely to exit the labour market. Husbands' public sector employment tends to prevent women from exiting from the labour force.

It seems important that women kept a good stable job (i.e. being schoolteachers) and were able to receive social support (i.e. co-residence with parents and family-friendly husbands' workplace) for their continued employment. Among these factors, it should be noted that parents' support is not accessible by anybody at any time. Even when women live near their parents at the birth of the first child, there is a good possibility that their parents will not live nearby thereafter due to relocation of women or their families, or worsened health condition or death of their parents. If women's continued employment is dependent on their parents' support, it can be said that the basis of women's continued employment is rather weak, even for those women who have been able to remain in the labour force beyond the birth of the first child.

Table 6.5 Discrete-time event history models predicting labour force exit after the birth of the first child

	Coef.	Exp(B)
Time		
The year of birth to 1 year since birth	–	–
2–3 years since birth	0.369	1.447
4–5 years since birth	−0.348	0.706
6–9 years since birth	−0.670	0.512
10–14 years since birth	−1.577	0.207
15 years or over since birth	−2.233	0.107
Educational attainment		
Junior high school or high school	–	–
Junior college	−0.190	0.827
University	0.002	1.002
Unemployment rate	0.295	1.343
Birth cohort		
1960s	–	–
1970s	−0.199	0.820
Age at the first birth	−0.034	0.966
First occupation		
Professional	−0.202	0.817
Clerical	–	–
Service and sales	0.462	1.589
Manual labour	0.539	1.714
Self-employed	−1.015	0.362
Teaching	−1.110[†]	0.330
Residence distance from parents		
Co-residence	−1.042 **	0.353
Proximate residence	−0.574	0.563
Parents lived further away than the same town, parents deceased	–	–
Husband's income	0.00001	1.000
Husband's public-sector employment	−1.019*	0.361
Number of children	0.183	1.200
Age of youngest child	0.088	1.091
Constant	−3.001	
Log likelihood	−271.753	
Person-year spells, n	2099	
LR χ^2 (d.f.)	49.90 (21)	
Prob > χ^2	0.000	

Source: JPSC.

Note: Analysis was conducted for women who were in the labour force at the year of the first childbirth.

[†]$p < .10$, *$p < .05$, **$p < .01$, ***$p < .001$.

Summary: Career-building after childbirth

Trends in women's re-entry to the labour force

Around 70% of women born in the 1960s and the 1970s were not employed at the birth of the first child. However, by the time their first child reached school age, about half of them were employed. The 1970s cohort re-entered the labour market earlier than the 1960s cohort. The year-by-year analysis of the changes in their employment status during 10 years after the birth of the first child showed that women experienced various changes during these years. That is, there were a certain number of women who exited the labour market or who experienced changes in their employment status, as well as those who re-entered the labour market.

Women who were not employed at the birth of the first child began to re-enter the labour force 5 years after the birth, and the survival rate of staying outside the labour force was 40%–50% and 20%–25% at the tenth and fifteenth year after the birth, respectively. Compared to women whose first position was as clerical workers, those who were professionals or self-employed workers were more likely to re-enter the labour market, as was true of those who co-resided or lived near their parents compared to those who resided far from them. Moreover, a higher husband's income and lower age of their youngest child related to lower probability of women's re-entry. When all these factors were controlled for, no difference was observed between the cohorts.

Women's careers after their re-entry to the labour market

The subsequent work career of women who re-entered the labour market has been unexplored in research of women's work careers. Given that women's work careers do not end when they re-enter the labour market, this chapter has examined the possibility of career-building after women's re-entrance to the labour market and the factors that hinder it.

It is the current reality that many women re-enter the labour market as non-regular employees. In the data analysed in this chapter, this was true of an overwhelming majority of women (75%). The percentage of these women who remain as non-regular employees is estimated at 45% and 25% in the fifth and tenth year, respectively. In other words, the data suggest that these women experience further changes in their employment status quite soon after their re-entry to the labour market, and many of these women exit the labour market altogether.

This chapter also examined, among the women who re-entered the labour market as non-regular employees, what kinds of women experienced changes in their employment status and what changes they were. Women who re-entered the labour market as non-regular sales or service workers were less likely to become regular employees or self-employed workers compared to those who did so as clerical workers. Moreover, women are more likely to exit the labour force while their youngest child is still young.

Risk of exit from the labour market for women who were employed at the birth of the first child

This chapter further analysed the risk of exit from the labour market for women who were employed at the birth of the first child. Among such women, 87.7%, 77.0% and 69.2% of them remained employed at the fifth, tenth and fifteenth year after the birth, respectively. This was probably because their occupational and family conditions were favourable, allowing them to remain in the labour force. When women have favourable conditions that allow them to remain in the labour market in the same year as the birth of the first child, there is a high possibility that they are able to remain employed thereafter; however, this is not true for many women in present-day Japan.

I examined factors that increased the risk of exit from the labour force even for these women. The results presented earlier showed that those whose first occupation was as a schoolteacher were less likely to exit the labour force than those whose first job was as a clerical worker, and those who co-resided with their parents and those whose husbands were employed by the public sector were less likely to do so.

Human resource development systems in the Japanese firm-specific internal labour market and women's careers after childbirth

What do these findings suggest? Women's educational attainment has little utility as part of human capital in the career-building of post-partum women. Instead, their occupation was found to have a significant effect on their various post-childbirth career-building phases. Women's educational attainment can impact on the types of occupations they can enter at the beginning of their career. However, it was not found to increase their probability of re-entering the labour market or to facilitate subsequent changes in their employment status from non-regular to regular employment.

The fact that the type of women's occupations, rather than their educational attainment, has a significant impact on their post-birth career-building phases implies that few positions are available at many Japanese firms where women who have exited the labour market for childbirth or child rearing can rebuild their career. Women whose first occupation was as a clerical worker are less likely to re-enter the labour market than those who began their career as professionals or self-employed workers. This is probably because in the Japanese firm-specific labour market, only men receive on-the-job training and tasks with responsibilities, on the assumption that only they will remain in the labour market for the long term. It can also be inferred that female clerical workers are not given opportunities to acquire skills that facilitate their long-term career-building in the first place, and not many positions themselves are available for women where they can resume their career after the birth of a child.

Many women who have failed to be included in the Japanese firm-specific internal labour market re-enter the labour market as non-regular sales or service workers. However, when they do so, they will find it difficult to receive opportunities that will lead them to become regular employees or self-employed workers. Subsequent career options are also very limited for them.

Given these realities, what we need in light of Japanese women's post-partum career-building is to generate positions and career routes where women who have exited the labour market for childbirth or child rearing can rebuild their career within the system of task and personnel allocation in firms. According to recent media reports, some firms have set up re-employment systems for post-partum women, while others have set up systems to promote experienced non-regular employees to 'limited regular employees' who are not required to transfer among different regions.[1] These movements deserve acclaim, as they will generate the positions and routes for women discussed earlier, and close attention should be paid to their future results.

The ongoing choice between child rearing or work, after re-entry to the labour market

In addition to these issues on the demand side of the labour market for post-partum women, the results from this chapter shed light on the fact that the burden of child rearing is mostly shouldered by mothers and there is a lack of support for women regarding household chores and child rearing.

The result that a younger age of their youngest child decreases women's likelihood of re-entering the labour market suggests that women with younger children cannot work outside the home because more of their time has to be devoted to child rearing and household chores. In other words, their decision to re-enter the labour market is made only when they see themselves able to also manage child rearing and household chores. Moreover, even after they re-enter the labour market as non-regular employees, they are more likely to exit the labour market when their youngest child is very young. This implies that while their child is young, women find it difficult to work while managing child rearing and household chores, and when they have a second or third child, they have to devote themselves to child rearing again, consequently finding themselves with no choice but to leave the labour market. In sum, since mainly women are responsible for child rearing, they are confronted with the choice between child rearing or work even after they re-enter the labour market.

Re-examination of the importance of parents' support

Since women shoulder most of the burden of child rearing and household chores, their parents are playing an important role as a major source of support for working women by helping them in their child rearing and household chores. Co-residing with parents or living near them not only increases the chance of women's re-entrance to the labour market but also decreases the risk of exit from the labour market of those women who are employed at the birth of the first child. Together with the discussion outlined in Chapter 5, this finding suggests that being able to receive support from parents by living near them has a significant positive effect on women's employment shortly after the birth of a child, as well as during the child-rearing and post-child-rearing years.

Now, let me consider the meaning of this support's ongoing effect on women's employment. First, parents are either directly related to the women or their husbands. They are limited resources that cannot be accessed by anyone at any time. The availability of this resource depends not only on the residence distance between women and the parents but also on the parents' health status and employment condition, as well as women's relationship with them. Moreover, even if they are available at a given point in time, there is no guarantee that they will remain so, as there is a high possibility that they will suddenly become unavailable due to relocation of the women and their family or worsening health conditions of the parents. If women's re-entrance to the labour market and continuous employment past the birth of the first child are made possible only by support from their parents, the basis of their employment may be more fragile than they expect. It is now time for us to realise the importance of discussing the allocation of childcare support in society.

Note

1 Newspaper *Nikkei* reported that Ito Yokado, one of the major retail companies, introduced the status of 'limited regular employees' which required no transfer among different regions in their personnel allocation systems (*Nikkei*, 2013, December 3, p. 1).

References

Higuchi, Yoshio. 2000. Paneru dēta ni yoru josei no kekkon, shussan, shūgyō no dōgaku bunseki (A dynamic analysis of women's marriage, childbirth, and employment using panel data). *Gendai Keizaigaku no Choryu,* 109–148.

Higuchi, Yoshio. 2007. Josei no shūgyō keizoku shiensaku (Social policy on women's employment continuation). *Mita Business Review,* 50(5): 45–66.

Hirao, Keiko. 2005. Josei no gakureki to saishūshoku (Who returns to the labour market?). *Japanese Journal of Family Sociology,* 17(1): 34–43.

Honda, Kazunari. 2010. *Shufu pāto saidai no hiseiki koyō* (Wives' part-time employment, the largest share of non-regular employment). Tokyo: Shueisha.

Nishimura, Junko. 2009. *Posuto ikujiki no josei to hatarakikata: wāku famirī baransu to sutoresu* (Women and work in post childcare stage: Work-family balance and stress). Tokyo: Keio University Press.

Sakamoto, Yuka. 2009. Jinteki shihon no chikuseki to daiisshi shussango no saishūshoku katei (The effect of the human capital accumulation on women's re-employment). *Journal of the National Women's Education Center of Japan,* 13: 59–71.

Yamato, Reiko. 2011. Josei no M jigata raifu kōsu no nikkan hikaku (Japan-Korea comparison of women's M-shaped life course). In Yoshimichi Sato & Fumiaki Ojima (Eds.), *Gendai no kaiso shakai 1* (The contemporary stratification society, 1) (pp. 161–175). Tokyo: University of Tokyo Press.

7 Careers of Japanese single mothers

Characteristics of Japanese single mothers

The increasing number of single mothers and their tough economic circumstances

The number of single mothers in Japan is increasing. According to the Nationwide Survey on Fatherless Families, conducted continuously by the Ministry of Health, Labour and Welfare, the number of single-mother households was estimated at approximately 630,000 in 1978, increasing to 950,000 in 1998 and reaching 1.23 million in the latest survey conducted in 2011.

Many single-mother households are facing tough economic circumstances. The Nationwide Survey on Fatherless Families in 2011 showed that in 2010, the average annual earned income of mothers in single-mother households was 1.81 million yen, and 64% of mothers in single-mother households earned less than 2 million yen per year. The average household income of single-mother households including social security payments (childcare allowance, etc.), child support from ex-husbands and allowance money from their parents, in addition to wages, was 2.91 million yen, or just about 40% of the average income of households with children, which was 6.58 million yen according to the Comprehensive Survey of Living Conditions in 2011 (Ministry of Health, Labour and Welfare, Japan, 2012).

Long working hours have not eased economic situations

The employment rate among single mothers is quite high. According to the Nationwide Survey on Fatherless Families of 2011, 80.6% of mothers in single-mother households were in the labour force at the time of the survey. Another study has also reported that such single mothers work as many as an average of 39 hours per week (Zhou, 2008).

This combination of a high employment rate and a high poverty rate with low income is considered characteristic of Japanese single mothers. The poverty rate of single-mother households where the mother works is as high as 58% in Japan, the highest among OECD countries (OECD, 2008). Considering that the main reason for single-mother poverty in other countries is lack of jobs, it is peculiar that single mothers with jobs live in poverty in Japan.

Public-income transfer methods, the low payout rate of child support from ex-husbands and their low rates of earned income all contribute to the tough economic circumstances faced by single mothers (Oishi, 2012a). Single mothers probably work for low hourly wages, and this makes it hard for them to earn enough to support themselves and their children. In fact, 52.1% of working single mothers were non-regular employees – for instance, part-time workers and dispatched workers – in 2011, according to the Nationwide Survey on Fatherless Families. It has been reported that female temporary workers earn 50.5 yen for every 100 yen earned by male general workers (Cabinet Office, Government of Japan, 2013), so there is a wage gap between men and women and between regular and non-regular employees. Therefore, many single mothers who are non-regular employees cannot earn enough income to support themselves and their children.

Research questions

This chapter examines the working careers of single mothers from two per-spectives: opportunities to move from non-regular employee positions to regular employment and the risk of exit from the labour force. In Japan, there are disparities between regular and non-regular employees in job secu-rity, opportunities for training, availability of a safety net (e.g. social secu-rity programmes) and wages. Regular employment positions can facilitate an economically secure life for single mothers. Moreover, for single moth-ers, continuous employment is essential for living. However, we can easily imagine how difficult it is for women to remain in the labour force while raising children. Therefore, this chapter also examines factors that heighten the risk of job resignation for single mothers and clarifies conditions that hamper their continuous employment.

Previous research on working careers of Japanese single mothers

Little research has been conducted on the working careers of single moth-ers. One reason is lack of data that allows investigation of their careers over time. Nevertheless, this section first summarises previous studies' findings on the careers of single mothers and the factors affecting them. Nagase (2003) compared employment rates of single mothers and married women with children by using data from the Employment Status Survey of 1997, finding that although having children curbed employment of both single mothers and married women, the effect was smaller for single mothers.

Oishi (2012b) found two factors preventing single mothers from being regular employees: having children of preschool age and the poor health conditions of the mothers themselves. Zhou (2012) also showed that the age of the youngest child (6 or above) and single mothers' holding of professional qualifications, such as in nursing, cooking and care work, were factors in their regular employment.

Using data from the Labour Force Surveys between 1990 and 2009, Sato (2011) observed that single mothers who were heads of households were less likely to become regular employees than heads of two-parent households. In addition, Yuzawa, Fujiwara and Ishida (2012) examined data on qualified recipients of child-rearing allowances in a municipality from 2002 and 2006. This data did not include all single-mother households because it was based only on those who qualified for assistance. Although 73.3% of them were employed in 2005, only 39.4% were employed in all years from 2002 to 2006. This suggests that single mothers probably remained in the labour force through repeated resignations, job changes and re-entries into the labour force.

Changes in careers after becoming single mothers

This section focuses on women who became single mothers due to separation, divorce or death of their spouses during the study period. Therefore, unmarried mothers were not included in the study, although their number is gradually increasing among single-mother households.

Data from the JPSC for the years 1993 to 2008 included 160 women who divorced or separated from their spouses and 16 whose spouses died during the study period. Seven of those who separated from their spouses did so twice. None experienced both separation/divorce and the death of a spouse. This section examines the working careers of women who had at least one child at the time of their first separation/divorce or their spouse's death (n = 134).

The average age of women at the time of separation/divorce or spouse's death was 34.61 years. Since the standard deviation was 5.20, the data included many women who became single mothers in their thirties. At the time of separation/divorce or spouse's death, 37%, 40% and 23% of the women had one, two and three or more children, respectively. The average age of their youngest child was 7.02 years, and about 50% of the women had children under 6 years old at the time of the separation/divorce or spouse's death. Therefore, many single mothers included in the data were in the middle of their child-rearing years. In the year of becoming a single mother, 35%, 40% and 4% of the women were regular employees, non-regular employees and self-employed workers, respectively; 21% of them were outside the labour force.

Women's employment status in the decade after becoming single mothers

Table 7.1 shows the employment status of these women during the decade after becoming single mothers. For those who remarried during the study period, data after remarriage were excluded. Since the data covered only a 16-year period (1993–2008), the sample size decreased with the passage of time after becoming a single mother. The percentage information beyond 6 years after becoming a single mother is given for reference only because the sample size decreased significantly after that point.

Table 7.1 shows that the percentage of women who were regular employees in the year of separation/divorce or spouse's death was 35%, but it increased to 44% 5 years later. This suggests that some women who became single mothers changed their employment status from non-regular employment to regular employment for financial security, and others who were not working when they became single mothers entered the labour market as regular employees. The percentage of women who worked as non-regular employees remained approximately 40% through-out the 5-year period after they became single mothers. Not many of the women were self-employed in any of these years. Around 20% of the women were not working in the year when they became single mothers, but the number decreased slightly, to 15%, by 5 years after separation/ divorce or spouse's death.

Changes in women's employment status during the decade after becoming single mothers

Table 7.2 shows changes in the women's employment status during the 10-year period after they became single mothers. The percentage of women who remained regular employees from the year of separation/divorce or death of spouse until the end of the first year after that life event was 27%, but it increased to 39.6% by the fourth and fifth years. Similarly, the per-centage of women who remained non-regular employees from the year of separation/divorce or death of spouse until the end of the first year after that life event was 29.7%, and it increased to 35.4% in the fourth and fifth

Table 7.1 Distribution of women's employment status during the decade after separation/divorce or death of spouse

(%)

	The year of separation/ divorce or death of spouse	1 year after separation/ divorce or death of spouse	2 years	3 years	4 years	5 years	6 years	7 years	8 years	9 years	10 years
Regular	35.1	39.6	37.8	40.5	42.6	43.8	37.8	43.8	50.0	42.1	47.1
Non-regular	40.3	44.1	44.9	44.3	44.3	37.5	48.7	31.3	21.4	36.8	29.4
Self-employed	3.7	1.8	3.1	3.8	3.3	4.2	2.7	12.5	14.3	5.3	11.8
Not employed	20.9	14.4	14.3	11.4	9.8	14.6	10.8	12.5	14.3	15.8	11.8
Total	100	100	100	100	100	100	100	100	100	100	100
N	134	111	98	79	61	48	37	32	28	19	17

Source: JPSC.

Note: Analysis was conducted for women with children at the year of separation/divorce or death of spouse.

Table 7.2 Changes in women's employment status in each year during the decade after separation/divorce or death of spouse

(%)

	0–1 year	1–2 years	2–3 years	3–4 years	4–5 years	5–6 years	6–7 years	7–8 years	8–9 years	9–10 years
Continued regular employment	27.0	31.6	36.4	32.8	39.6	35.1	32.3	42.9	42.1	41.2
Continued non-regular employment	29.7	36.7	32.9	36.1	35.4	37.8	29.0	14.3	21.1	29.4
Continued self-employment	0.9	2.0	1.3	3.3	4.2	2.7	3.2	14.3	5.3	5.9
Continued employment with a change in status	18.0	8.2	10.1	14.8	4.2	8.1	19.4	3.6	10.5	5.9
Getting employed	9.9	7.1	7.6	3.3	2.1	5.4	3.2	10.7	5.3	5.9
Resignation	4.5	7.1	3.8	1.6	6.6	0.0	0.0	7.1	5.3	0.0
Continued as being not employed	9.9	7.1	7.6	8.2	8.3	10.8	12.9	7.1	10.5	11.8
Total	100	100	100	100	100	100	100	100	100	100
N	111	98	79	61	48	37	31	28	19	17

Source: JPSC.

Note: Analysis was conducted for women with children at the year of separation/divorce or death of spouse.

years. In other words, the percentage of women who retained their employment status from the previous year increased with the passage of time. The percentage who experienced a change in employment status varied across the years, and in some years, it was 15% to 20%. Not many of the women moved from outside to within the labour force, but about 7% to 10% of them did so each year after becoming single mothers, until the third year, when the percentage then decreased with time. At most, only 7% of the women exited the labour force each year, and the percentage of women who remained outside the labour force from one year to the next was about 7% to 10% each year.

Tables 7.1 and 7.2 indicate the following: (1) Most single mothers were employed either as regular or as non-regular employees; (2) their employment rate was higher a few years after they became single mothers than it was immediately afterwards; (3) some women remained outside the labour market for 10 years after becoming single mothers; (4) and most changes in employment status (including from being outside to within the labour market) occurred soon after the women became single mothers, yet such changes continued to occur after that.

Opportunities for getting regular employment and risk of labour force exit

This section examines opportunities for single mothers to become regular employees since regular employment offers them financial stability. The section also examines the risk of labour force exit because it can cause tremendous financial harm to the lives of single mothers and their children, although the percentage of single mothers who exited the labour force was relatively small, as seen in Table 7.2.

Opportunities for getting regular employment

An event history analysis in single mothers' getting regular employment was conducted. Subjects were women who were non-regular employees, self-employed workers or those who were not employed in the year when they became single mothers ($N = 86$). According to the probability of getting regular employment, as calculated by the Kaplan-Meier method, the percentage who had not got regular employment by the fifth year after becoming a single mother was estimated at 68.8% (figure not shown). This suggests that women who are not regular employees when they become single mothers later experience difficulty in becoming regular employees.

Next, a discrete-time event history model was applied to examine the effect of factors on change in employment status to regular employment after women became single mothers. Independent variables analysed were women's educational attainment, their employment status when they became single mothers, distance of residence from parents, age of the youngest child and unemployment rate. Results are shown in Table 7.3. Appendix Table S.6 shows means and standard deviations. Since only 3 of the 86 women

Table 7.3 Discrete-time event history models predicting entry to regular employment for single mothers

	Coef.	*Exp(B)*
Time		
0 to 1 year since separation/divorce or death of spouse	–	–
2–4 years	−0.419	0.658
5 years or over	−0.342	0.710
Educational attainment		
Junior high school or high school	–	–
Junior college or university	−0.911	0.402
Unemployment rate	−0.153	0.858
Employment status at the year of separation/divorce or death of spouse		
Non-regular employee or self-employed	0.556	1.744
Not employed	–	–
Residence distance from parents		
Co-residence	1.115*	3.049
Proximate residence	1.005†	2.732
Parents lived further away than the same town, parents deceased	–	–
Age of youngest child	0.124**	1.132
Constant	3.519	
Log likelihood	−91.517	
Person-year spells, n	406	
LR χ^2 (d.f.)	15.50 (8)	
Prob > χ^2	0.050	

Source: JPSC.

Note: Analysis was conducted for single mothers who were either non-regular employees, self-employed or not employed at the year of separation/divorce or death of spouse.

$^†p < .10$, $^*p < .05$, $^{**}p < .01$, $^{***}p < .001$.

included in this analysis graduated from university or higher, the category of university or higher and that of junior college, technical or vocational school were merged. Note that as Fujiwara (2012) observed, some attention should be paid to the fact that single mothers tend to have lower educational levels, and this relates to a lower regular employment rate and lower income from work.

Table 7.3 indicates that age of youngest child and distance of residence from parents showed significant impact on change in employment status to regular employment. Women whose youngest child was older were more likely to become regular employees. Conversely, this means that women with a young child found it harder to become regular employees. Co-residence or proximate residence to parents facilitates change to regular employment.

Risk of labour force exit

Next, an event history analysis was conducted to examine the risk of labour force exit after the woman became a single mother. The analysis included women in the labour force when they became single mothers regardless of employment status (regular, non-regular, self-employed, etc.) (N=106). The result of the Kaplan-Meier method indicates that the percentage of women who had stayed in the labour market until the fifth year after becoming a single mother was estimated at 75%. This shows that the rate of continuous employment after the women became single mothers was high. Next, a discrete-time event history model was applied to examine the effect of factors on probability of labour force exit after the women became single mothers. Independent variables included were women's employment status (whether the women were in regular employment), distance of residence from parents, age of the youngest child, unemployment rate and remarriage (occurred or not). Appendix Table S.7 shows means and standard deviations.

Table 7.4 shows that while age of the youngest child and non-regular employment or self-employment negatively affected exit risk, the unemployment rate and remarriage positively affected labour force exit. These results show the difficulty that single mothers have in staying in the labour force, and due to this constraint, single mothers are often the first to be laid off when the economy is bad and unemployment rate is high. The negative impact of non-regular jobs or self-employment in the year of separation/ divorce or spouse's death on labour force exit is seemingly at odds with the prediction; however, it implies difficulty for single mothers remaining in regular employment. Furthermore, the positive effect of remarriage on labour force exit suggests that marriage is still strongly related to gender roles in the division of labour.

Table 7.4 Discrete-time event history models predicting labour force exit for single mothers

	Coef.	*Exp(B)*
Time		
0 to 1 year since separation/divorce or death of spouse	–	–
2–4 years	0.837	2.309
5 years or over	0.678	1.970
Educational attainment		
Junior high school or high school	–	–
Junior college	–0.308	0.735
University	–1.776	0.170
Unemployment rate	1.182*	3.259
Employment status at the year of separation/divorce or death of spouse		
Regular employee	–	–
Non-regular employee or self-employed	–1.253*	0.286
Residence distance from parents		
Co-residence	–0.604	0.547
Proximate residence	–1.320†	0.267
Parents lived further away than the same town, parents deceased	–	–
Age of youngest child	–0.163*	0.850
Got remarried	4.378***	79.690
Constant	–7.041	
Log likelihood	–68.365	
Person-year spells, n	520	
LR χ^2 (d.f.)	51.68	
Prob > χ^2	0.000	

Source: JPSC.

Note: Analysis was conducted for single mothers who were working at the year of separation/divorce or death of spouse.

†$p < .10$, *$p < .05$, **$p < .01$, ***$p < .001$.

Summary: working careers of single mothers and Japanese employment practices

This section examined the working careers of women who became single mothers after separation/divorce or the death of a spouse. Most data were from women who became single mothers when their youngest child was under 6 years old; therefore, it was possible to examine the determining factors in the careers of single mothers during their child-rearing years. Of course, because the JPSC did not target only single mothers, the sample size was quite small. This limitation notwithstanding, the analysis provided some important findings for discussing greater career security for single mothers.

Regular employment: Incompatibility with single mothers' lives

The analysis of this chapter confirmed a high employment rate for single mothers: around 80% of women included in the study were in the labour market when they became single mothers. However, the percentage of women who were non-regular employees was also high.

This chapter examined the working careers of single mothers from two perspectives. The first analysis examined the likelihood of women who were non-regular employees, self-employed workers or not employed when they became single mothers becoming regular employees. An event history analysis showed that having young children prevents single mothers becoming regular employees, indicating that in Japanese society today, raising young children as a single mother is incompatible with working as a regular employee. This is probably because Japanese regular employees are made to work long hours in return for high wages and job security. Yamaguchi (2009) noted that compared with non-regular employees, regular employees in Japan are more likely to encounter excessive work, such as working on non-work days, working overtime or working full-time while hoping not to work or to work only part-time. He argued that this is because regular employees work long hours and because companies tend to reject regular employees' requests for shorter working hours. In other words, short working hours are generally not allowed for regular employees in Japan. In addition, workers must follow their companies' decisions about working overtime; their individual circumstances are not considered. These working conditions are obviously obstacles for single mothers with young children.

Peripheral positions in the labour market and their consequences

This chapter's analysis also found that single mothers' risk of labour force exit decreased with the increasing age of the youngest child and increased with the unemployment rate and remarriage. Having young children not only inhibits single mothers from obtaining a regular employment position but also increases the risk of labour force exit. This suggests that child rearing by single mothers is sometimes incompatible with working, and they sometimes have no choice but to quit their jobs. Moreover, when the unemployment rate is high and the economy is bad, workers are believed to refrain from resigning since finding a new job is hard under such conditions. However, employers are expected to encourage their employees to resign in order to reduce labour costs, and this action is more likely to affect single mothers. That is, single mothers are the first to be laid off when the unemployment rate is high and the economy is bad, implying that single mothers are peripheral actors in the labour market. This chapter's analysis also showed that remarriage increases the likelihood of single mothers quitting their jobs. This may also be related to the peripheral positions that single mothers hold in the labour market. Single mothers may have little or no motivation to keep their jobs without opportunities for career development when their economic conditions are improved through remarriage. At the same time, however, this means that these women are again placed into gender roles in the division of labour, thus closing the door to their financial independence. The institution of marriage itself, even remarriage, seems strongly related to the gender division of labour.

Employment practices in the firm-specific internal labour market that hinder single mothers' employment

In Japan, good, stable jobs are given only to regular employees; yet, in return, regular employees are made to work long hours. These characteristics, specific to the Japanese firm-specific internal labour market, hinder single mothers' employment. Single mothers with young children cannot work long hours, although working long hours is often associated with regular employment, so many have no choice but to work as non-regular employees. However, non-regular employment is unstable for single mothers because when the economy worsens, they are often forced to resign. Moreover, these positions have no future prospects. All these factors keep single mothers' earned income low, although their employment rate is high. Loosening the tight link between stable jobs with benefits and long working hours would contribute to improving the lives of Japanese single mothers. Furthermore, loosening that link probably offers benefits not only to single mothers. Since good, stable jobs are provided only in return for long working hours, a great number of people in Japan are probably accepting a way of working that is not what they would prefer.

References

Cabinet Office, Government of Japan. 2013. *Danjo kyōdō sankaku hakusho Heisei 25 nenban* (White paper on gender equality 2014). Tokyo: Author. Retrieved from http://www.gender.go.jp/about_danjo/whitepaper/h25/zentai/index.html#pdf (accessed July 29, 2015).

Fujiwara, Chisa. 2012. Boshisetai no hinkon to gakureki (Poverty and educational attainment among single-female-parent household). *Gendaishiso*, 40(15): 158–165.

Ministry of Health, Labour and Welfare, Japan. 2012. *Heisei 23 nen kokumin seikatsu kiso chōsa no gaikyō* (Report on Comprehensive Survey of Living Condition 2011). Retrieved from http://www.mhlw.go.jp/toukei/saikin/hw/k-tyosa/k-tyosa11/dl/12.pdf (accessed February 7, 2014).

Ministry of Health, Labour and Welfare, Japan. Various years. *Zenkoku boshisetai tō chōsa* (Nationwide Survey on Fatherless Families). Retrieved from http://www.mhlw.go.jp/toukei/list/86–1.html (accessed February 7, 2014).

Nagase, Nobuko. 2003. Boshi setai no haha no kyaria keisei, sono kanōsei (Career development and its possibility of mothers in single-female-parent households). In Japan Institute of Labour (Ed.), *Boshi setai no haha heno shūgyō shien ni kansuru kenkyū* (Research on employment support for mothers in single-female-parent households) (pp. 239–289). Tokyo: Japan Institute of Labour.

OECD. 2008. *Growing unequal?: Income distribution and poverty in OECD countries*. Paris: OECD.

Oishi, Akiko. 2012a. Boshi setai ha hataraite itemo naze hinkon ka (Why are mothers in single-female-parent households in poverty although they are working?). *Shukan Shakaihosho*, 2705: 50–55.

Oishi, Akiko. 2012b. Hiseiki shūgyō ga boshi setai no hinkon to seifuthi netto karano datsuraku ni oyobosu eikyō (Impact of non-regular employment on poverty and dropout of safety nets among mothers in single-female-parent households). In JILPT (Ed.), *Shinguru mazā no shūgyō to keizaiteki jiritsu* (Employment and financial independence of single mothers) (pp. 79–98). Tokyo: JILPT.

Sato, Tetsuaki. 2011. Hi jōko kara seiki jōko heno tankan: boshi setai no haha ha furi nanoka (Transition from non-regular to regular employment: Are mothers in single-female-parent households disadvantaged?). *Mita Journal of Economics*, 103(4): 601–618.

Yamaguchi, Kazuo. 2009. *Wāku raifu baransu* (Work–life balance). Tokyo: Nikkei.

Yuzawa, Naomi, Chisa Fujiwara, & Hiroshi Ishida. 2012. Boshi setai no shotoku hendō to shokugyō idō (Change in income and occupation among single-female-parent households). *Social Policy and Labor Studies*, 4(1): 97–110.

Zhou, Yanfei. 2008. Ankēto chōsa: haha ni kiku shigoto to seikatsu to shien ni tsuite (Survey: Asking mothers about work, life and support). In JILPT (Ed.), *Boshi setai no haha heno shūgyō shien ni kansuru kenkyū* (Research on employment support for mothers in single-female-parent households) (pp. 165–207). Tokyo: JILPT.

Zhou, Yanfei. 2012. Boshi setai no hahaoya ni okeru seishain shūgyō no jōken (Factors of regular employment for mothers in single-female-parent households). *The Quarterly of Social Security Research*, 48(3): 319–333.

8 Conclusion

Findings of this study

The Japanese economy experienced a severe recession from the 1990s to the early 2000s. During this period, the structure of the labour market was transformed, the fertility rate dropped and policies to facilitate women's employment were implemented. This study examined the employment of women born in the 1960s and 1970s who experienced childbirth and raised children during this period. The employment behaviour of these women before and after childbirth through the post-child-rearing period and the working careers of single mothers during the period were examined. The findings from each chapter are as follows.

Chapter 1 showed that labour supply factors by themselves cannot explain women's participation in the labour force in Japan and that it is necessary to examine how labour supply is conditioned by labour demand. From that standpoint, this study aimed to elucidate the effects of interaction between the Japanese firm-specific internal labour market and social policies on women's employment.

In Chapter 2, changes in the M-shaped curve were examined to demonstrate that relationships between life events, such as marriage and childbirth, and women's employment cannot be inferred from the M-shaped curve itself.

Chapter 3 considered the research framework of this study. The chapter examined effects from the economic recession during the 1990s and the early 2000s on the firm-specific internal labour market and on employment practices, which in turn are thought to have greatly influenced Japanese women's employment. The firm-specific internal labour market shrank in the 1990s and the early 2000s, making the entry into the labour market more competitive. Meanwhile, the number of non-regular employees increased (especially among younger workers), and employment practices particular to Japan survived in the firm-specific internal labour market.

On the other hand, the fertility rate declined and social policies to support women's employment began to be implemented after the 1990s. As a result of such policies, the social security benefits provided to households with children improved. Presumably, however, the policies are not enough to facilitate women's participation in the labour force because the labour market does not favour employment for women.

In Chapter 4, results from descriptive analyses of the employment rate of women after marriage and childbirth and the continuous employment rate from before marriage to after childbirth were presented. Women's employment rate at marriage in the 1940s birth cohort was slightly below 50%, but it was well over 50%, slightly over 60% and around 70% in the 1950s, 1960s and 1970s birth cohorts, respectively. Furthermore, the employment rate can vary depending on analysis period and the rate's denominator. The continuous employment rate from the year before marriage until marriage among the 1960s and 1970s birth cohorts was over 60%, but the rate from the year before marriage to the year after marriage was 40%. Moreover, the continuous regular employment rate from the year before marriage to the year after marriage was only about 25% for the 1960s and 1970s birth cohorts. This suggests that although younger women are more likely to work after marriage, it does not mean they work continuously as regular employees after they marry. On the other hand, the number of non-regular employees is increasing among the young, and the continuous regular employment rate from the year before marriage to the year after marriage was only 25% to 30%, even among the 1970s birth cohort.

The employment rate and regular employment rate of women 1 year after the birth of their first child were around 25% to 30% and 10% to 15%, respectively, among those born from the 1940s to the 1970s. That is, for women born in these periods, although the employment rate at marriage increased in younger generations, not much difference in employment behaviour after giving birth was observed across generations. It cannot be said that younger women were more likely to work regardless of childbirth.

Chapter 5 explored factors in women's employment during childbirth and child-rearing years under the labour market and social policy conditions discussed in Chapter 3. Results showed that only women who had professional careers, taught in schools, worked in public offices or were regular employees were able to remain in the labour market after the birth of their first child and for a period of 10 years afterwards. Schools and hospitals, where many teachers and professionals work, and public offices are thought to accommodate employees with family responsibilities. Such positions often require professional qualifications and therefore tend to offer stable employment. Only women who can find such jobs and/or work at such workplaces can remain in the labour market after childbirth.

An increasing number of women have been employed as non-regular employees, whereas women's career development in the firm-specific internal labour market has remained difficult. As a result, an increase in the continuous employment rate of women during the child-rearing years has yet to be seen. It seems important that women be employed as regular workers in order for them to remain in the labour market during their child-rearing years. However, regular employees in private firms are compelled to prioritise work over family life, so such work is not suitable for women with children. Hence, many women who work as regular employees do so in public offices or are professional workers at schools or hospitals. There have been fewer opportunities for women to be regular employees because regular employment positions in the labour market has shrunk since the 1990s. Therefore, women's continuous participation in the labour force during their child-rearing years remains difficult. Although social policies that support women's employment, such as childcare leave, began to be implemented during the 1990s and 2000s, they are not enough to support workers in private firms that require rigid work schedules. Moreover, the benefits of such social policies are available only to regular workers in many cases. Consequently, these policies have not yet increased women's continuous employment rate.

Chapter 6 examined the working careers of women born in the 1960s and 1970s after childbirth and through the post-child-rearing period. About 70% were outside the labour force in the year of their first child's birth; yet half of them were employed by the time their first child started school. The type of occupation before childbirth and family-related factors, such as distance of residence from parents, husband's income and age of the youngest child, affected these women's decisions about re-entry into the labour market. Women who began their careers as professional or technical workers and those who were self-employed were more likely to re-enter the labour market than those whose first occupation was a clerical job. This is probably because no positions exist in the Japanese firm-specific internal labour market for women to redevelop their careers after leaving the labour force for childcare reasons.

Moreover, many women who left the firm-specific internal labour market re-enter the labour force as non-regular sales or service employees. However, once they re-enter the labour market as non-regular workers, they are less likely to experience changes in employment status that will benefit them in developing careers, such as a change from non-regular to regular employment or self-employment. Paths for their career development after re-entry are very limited.

Analyses in Chapters 5 and 6 further revealed that living with or near parents facilitates the employment of women straight after childbirth, their continuous employment after childbirth and their re-entry into the labour market. Receiving support from parents by living with or near them has great significance for women's employment. However, parents are limited as resources since the parents only of women themselves or of their husbands are considered to be acceptable, and such resources are not available to everyone. The supposition that women's employment greatly depends on support from parents requires further examination.

The working careers of single mothers were examined in Chapter 7. These mothers' employment rate was 80% or higher during the first decade after they became single. However, the analysis suggested that women who were not regular employees in the year that they became single mothers had difficulty becoming regular employees at a later stage. Furthermore, results showed that having young children not only limited opportunities for women to get regular employment but also heightened their risk of exit from the labour force. Single mothers face great challenges in raising young children during employment as regular workers, probably because Japanese regular employees are often made to work long hours in return for high wages and job security. Support from parents also appears to be an important way for single mothers to obtain regular employment status, helping them to manage the rigid work schedules that are typically involved.

In the section ahead, aspects of women's employment that have not changed for women born in the 1960s and 1970s are summarised. Then characteristics of the employment behaviour of women in these birth cohorts, who gave birth and began child rearing in the 1990s and early 2000s, are discussed.

What has not changed in Japanese women's employment?

First, the employment rate of women as a whole has increased but that of women with young children has remained low. Nearly 70% of women born in the 1960s and 1970s were outside the labour market in the year of their first childbirth.

Second, women's higher educational attainment did not facilitate their employment before and after their first child was born for those in the 1960s or 1970s birth cohort. Moreover, educational attainment did not facilitate women's re-entry into the labour market.

Third, the percentage of women who were employed as non-regular employees while their first child was still very young (up to 2 years old) was only around 10% among both 1960s and 1970s birth cohorts. This showed that many women opted to stay outside the labour force rather than working as non-regular employees during that period, and they gradually re-entered the labour force as non-regular workers when their children grew a little older.

Increased number of non-regular employees and women's employment

At first glance, not much appears to have changed in the employment of women born in the 1960s and 1970s when their employment is compared with that of women from older generations. However, further examination revealed that employment of women born in the 1960s and 1970s during the child-rearing years has become even more difficult because the number of non-regular employees in the labour market has increased, while obstacles to entry into the firm-specific internal labour market have remained in place.

First, the increased number of non-regular employees among the young had an especially negative effect on women's continuous employment during the child-rearing years. As clarified by the analysis presented in Chapter 5, pre-pregnancy regular employment had positively affected women's continuous employment after childbirth. This is because in the Japanese labour market, only regular employees can expect pay raises and promotions commensurate with their length of service and only such employees can utilise company-specific child-rearing support systems (childcare leave in excess of that required by law, shorter working hours, etc.). On the other hand, non-regular employees can expect only a small economic return from remaining in the labour force. Many cannot utilise their companies' child-rearing support systems and therefore choose to exit the labour force after having a child. Consequently, the increased number of non-regular employees among the young has curbed women's increased employment rate during childbirth and child-rearing years.

Second, the increased number of non-regular employees in the labour market has even weakened the effect of women's higher educational attainment on their employment during child-rearing years. Since the employment situation was especially poor when women born in the 1970s graduated from university, this cohort has an especially high percentage of university-educated women working as non-regular employees. Since pre-pregnancy non-regular employment makes it difficult for women to remain in the labour force after childbirth, the effect of university education on continuous employment is less visible. Therefore, young women cannot expect higher educational attainment to be linked with good jobs and regular employment. In turn, this makes employment more difficult for women with higher education during their child-rearing years.

Women who raised their children from the 1990s to the early 2000s did so while obstacles to entry into the firm-specific internal labour market remained in place and the number of non-regular employees increased. Therefore, these women had increasing difficulty remaining in the labour market while raising their children. Some social policies to facilitate women's employment were implemented during this period, but many such policies provide support to women only while their children are very young. Moreover, many women in private firms find it difficult to manage work and family demands, even when they utilise the benefits of such policies, because of their inflexible work schedules. Furthermore, the system itself was targeted at regular workers, and consequently, new policies have not positively affected women's continuous employment because non-regular employment has become increasingly widespread among young women.

What is needed?

Transformation of the firm-specific internal labour market is needed to create a society where future generations of women can work while raising their children. For this to become a reality, this study suggests two measures. First, instead of providing workers with good, stable jobs in return for long working hours, the labour market needs to allow workers in such jobs to work flexible hours. Second, it is necessary to create paths that lead to good, stable jobs for those who choose to re-enter the labour market in the middle of their careers.

Flexible working hours for good, stable jobs

First, good, stable jobs are those that provide workers a sense of fulfilment and responsibility, opportunities for pay raises and promotions, job security and social security benefits. Under the present circumstances, jobs in the firm-specific internal labour market are considered good, stable jobs. However, workers with such jobs are made to work long hours and accept inflexible working schedules. As was especially apparent from the analysis of single mothers' working careers in Chapter 7, in Japan today, such jobs are equated with regular employment, and it is difficult for women to hold such jobs while raising young children. Jobs in public offices and professional jobs, such as teaching in a school and working in a hospital, are probably the few exceptions. Otherwise, most women born in the 1960s and 1970s had to resign from their jobs because of childbirth – even from jobs that were good and stable. This was probably because such jobs require long working hours that leave little time for child rearing. If flexible working hours were possible in stable jobs, women would be likely to keep such jobs while raising their children.

Relying on parents and barely managing

Allowing flexible hours for workers with stable jobs is considered the basis for child rearing. Results from this study showed that parents living with or close to working mothers provided them with long-term support during their careers. The support of parents was also important for the ability of single mothers to obtain regular employment. Parents are still important actors in child rearing even with the increased number of public childcare facilities. One reason is probably that women and men raising children in Japanese society have limited social networks from which they can draw support for child rearing. Such limited support comes solely from their parents. Women cannot expect to receive much help from their husbands, who work equally long or even longer hours. Moreover, it is not easy for women to build a childcare support network in their communities or to use commercial house-work and child-rearing services because of their costs and some normative considerations. (In Japan, it is believed that parents should be responsible for providing childcare, and many people are reluctant to allow strangers into their houses.) Therefore, the people whom women can rely on are limited, in a practical sense, to their own parents or their spouse's parents.

Another reason support from parents is essential for women's employment is that women cannot manage both work and child rearing without such support. Women need support from their parents when they cannot find any day-care providers, and even when they find one, they have to rely on their parents in case of last-minute (or frequent) requests for overtime or holiday work, or in the case of a sick child. Even after their children enter school, when they come home early, women sometimes need support from their parents since they cannot leave their children at home alone. Support from their parents in emergencies allows women (and of course men, too) to work. Conversely, this means that many people's current work circum-stances do not include provision for such situations. The relatively generous childcare leave system guaranteed by law can also be used only while chil-dren are still very young. For women who have older children, to accom-modate needs that arise suddenly or after normal business hours, Japanese firms should allow flexible working hours.

Day-care system for protecting children's rights

Although improving the day-care system is important for working parents, this goal should not be pursued with only the declining birth rate and men and women's work–life balance in mind. Improvements in the day-care system will guarantee children the right to receive early childhood educa-tion and care. Therefore, more day-care centres and preschools need to be built, and existing ones improved so that good childcare opportunities will be available to everyone. Under the integrated early childhood education and care scheme implemented in April 2015, the number of hours in day-care centres is determined by parents' working hours. After some discussion, it was decided that the system would allow regular childcare hours (11 hours per day) for parents working full-time and shorter childcare hours (8 hours per day) for parents working part-time. However, depending on the course of discussion, there are possible risks associated with having different childcare hours and different childcare arrival and departure times according to the parents' working hours.

However, the system of deciding childcare hours according to parents' working hours does not take into account that day-care centres do not simply provide a place for children to stay while their parents are working; they also provide social care and education. Through continuous accumulation of communication among children and solicitous care by caregivers, they can realise that they are different from others and that they and others are unique individuals. Through this experience, children can acquire skills for building relationships with others and cultivate motivation to attempt new things they could not do before – both fundamental capabilities to acquire before they start school. The system of determining childcare hours according to their parents' working hours does not consider these values of early childhood education and care, but even worse, they may allow children to stay in day-care centres for many hours, possibly neglecting children's fatigue and cutting back on the time that children and parents spend together, under the name of 'promotion of balancing work and family'.

Paths to good, stable jobs in the middle of careers

Paths should be created that lead to career-building jobs for people who choose to re-enter the labour market mid-career. The firm-specific internal labour market hires workers straight from school on the premise of lifetime employment. Workers are given on-the-job training and assigned new tasks at work so that they can acquire firm-specific skills and, in the future, become key figures within the company. As long as workers are on this path, they can continue to have a regular job with benefits. However, once they deviate from this path, the possibility of re-entering the firm-specific internal labour market closes. In many Japanese firms, there are no stable jobs or paths to rebuild careers for women who wish to re-enter the labour market after childbirth and child rearing. Only women who are professional, technical or self-employed workers can rebuild their careers after a hiatus since career-building paths in these occupations differ from those in the firm-specific internal labour market. If positions or paths to rebuild careers are created in various occupations, there will be more opportunities for women to utilise their human capital.

Such positions and paths are vital for those who cannot find a good, stable job and who become non-regular employees straight after school. People's careers should not be determined by their first jobs after completing their education. If opportunities to obtain good jobs are open to people in the middle of their careers, not only women who have experienced childbirth and child rearing but also all workers will benefit.

In this way, building paths to good jobs in mid-career should not be considered just as building a re-employment system for women who have left work due to childbirth and child rearing. Firms' reconsideration of assigning duties and evaluating performance in the labour market is needed so that a broader spectrum of people are able to find good mid-career jobs.

Prospects for change

One thing that can transform the firm-specific internal labour market and expand job opportunities for women is the severe labour shortage predicted for the 2010s. The size of the labour force in Japan is certainly decreasing. The birth rate is still declining, and the working-age population has been decreasing since the mid-1990s. In fact, in the early 1990s, Brinton (1993) predicted that labour shortages in the coming decade would create opportunities for women to remain in the labour force, even though the 1990s actually experienced a worsening of the employment scene for both men and women, resulting from the collapse of the bubble economy and subsequent long-term recession.

However, in the mid-2010s, due to the recovering economy as well as demographic factors, a labour shortage has become noticeable. The effective opening-to-application ratio was 1.0 in June 2015 (Ministry of Health, Labour and Welfare, Japan, 2015), suggesting that the demand for labour surpassed the supply. Since a chronic shortage of labour is expected in the future, Japanese firms are attempting to secure the necessary workers, and this practice can lead to changes in the firm-specific internal labour market and in employment practices within the market. One concrete example of such change is the promotion of non-regular employees to regular employees. In a survey on businesses (excluding businesses with less than 30 employees, public offices, agriculture, forestry and fishery) conducted by the JILPT in 2014, around half of businesses said that the number of regular employees would not change within 3 years, but 30% said that they were expecting some increase. Moreover, a system for promoting non-regular employees to regular employees was in place in about 35% of businesses (JILPT, 2015). This suggests that promotion of non-regular employees to regular employees is an important strategy for Japanese firms to secure their workforce.

Given that many Japanese women have been employed as non-regular employees, working without job security and being provided few opportunities for pay raises and promotions, the promotion of non-regular employees to regular employees can expand opportunities for women to work under better conditions. However, it is not that simple. When non-regular employees are promoted to regular employment, they often become 'limited regular employees'. Limited regular employees differ from regular employees in that their work locations are geographically limited, and the scope of their work is also limited. Although this way of working makes it easier to balance work and family life, there are disparities in wages and in prospects for promotions between regular employees and limited regular employees.

Turning the labour shortage and demographic crisis into greater job opportunities for women with children is a big task; however, considering the challenges that Japanese society faces in the future, that task is definitely worthwhile.

References

Brinton, Mary C. 1993. *Women and the economic miracle: Gender and work in postwar Japan.* Berkley: University of California Press.

JILPT. 2015. *Koyō pōtoforio no dōkō to hiseiki no seikikoyōka ni kansuru zantei repōto* (Temporary report on trends in employment and promotion of non-regular employees to regular employees). Tokyo: JILPT.

Ministry of Health, Labour and Welfare, Japan. 2015. *Ippan shokugyō shōkai jyōkyō* (Information on general employment placement). Retrieved from http://www.mhlw.go.jp/toukei/list/114–1.html (accessed August 3, 2015).

Appendix

Supplementary tables

Table S.1 Means and standard deviations of variables used in analyses of employment status at the year of the first childbirth

	1960s birth cohort				1970s birth cohort				1960s and 1970s birth cohort			
	Employed at 2 years before birth		*Regular employee at 2 years before birth*		*Employed at 2 years before birth*		*Regular employee at 2 years before birth*		*Employed at 2 years before birth*		*Regular employee at 2 years before birth*	
	(N = 717)		(N = 538)		(N = 503)		(N = 352)		(N = 117)		(N = 73)	
	Mean	*S.D.*	*Mean*	*S.D.*	*Mean*	*S.D.*	*Mean*	*S.D.*	*Mean*	*S.D.*	*Mean*	*S.D.*
Employed at the year of birth	0.349	0.477			0.346	0.476			0.393	0.491		
Regular employee at the year of birth			0.296	0.457			0.327	0.470			0.534	0.502
Educational attainment												
Junior high school or high school	0.531	0.499	0.550	0.498	0.457	0.499	0.438	0.497	0.291	0.456	0.247	0.434
Junior college	0.379	0.486	0.359	0.480	0.417	0.494	0.438	0.497	0.436	0.498	0.452	0.501
University	0.089	0.285	0.091	0.288	0.125	0.331	0.125	0.331	0.273	0.448	0.301	0.462
Year of the first childbirth												
1980s	0.368	0.482	0.400	0.490								
1990s	0.584	0.493	0.561	0.497	0.394	0.489	0.412	0.493				
2000s	0.047	0.212	0.039	0.194	0.606	0.489	0.588	0.493				
Unemployment rate, 2 years before birth	2.609	0.563	2.582	0.526	3.990	0.951	3.942	0.962	4.064	0.838	4.085	0.851
Birth cohort												
1960s									0.393	0.491	0.397	0.493
1970s									0.607	0.491	0.603	0.493

Age at first birth	30.667	2.767	31.000	3.087
Regular employee at 2 years before birth	0.624	0.486		
Firm size, 2 years before birth				
1–99	0.385	0.489	0.301	0.462
100–999	0.248	0.434	0.233	0.426
≥1000	0.171	0.378	0.205	0.407
Public sector employment	0.197	0.399	0.260	0.442
Occupation, 2 years before birth				
Professional			0.233	0.426
Clerical			0.411	0.496
Service and sales			0.137	0.346
Manual labour			0.082	0.277
Teaching			0.137	0.346
Residence distance from parents, 2 years before birth				
Co-residence	0.222	0.418	0.219	0.417
Proximate residence	0.068	0.253	0.068	0.254
Parents lived further away than the same town, parents deceased	0.709	0.456	0.712	0.456
Husband's annual income, 2 years before birth (10,000 yen)	443.291	366.041	466.219	449.442
Husband's public sector employment, 2 years before birth	0.154	0.362	0.178	0.385

Table S.2 Means and standard deviations of variables used in analyses of employment status 1 year after the first childbirth, and work continuation for 10 years after the first childbirth

	Employment 1 year after birth		Work continuation for 10 years after birth	
	(N = 483)		(N = 704)	
	Mean	S.D.	Mean	S.D.
Employed 1 year after birth	0.265	0.442		
Regular employee 1 year after birth	0.182	0.380		
Continue working for 10 years after first birth			0.158	0.365
Continue working as regular employee for 10 years after first birth			0.077	0.266
Educational attainment				
Junior high school or high school	0.342	0.475	0.544	0.498
Junior college	0.470	0.500	0.371	0.483
University	0.188	0.391	0.085	0.279
Unemployment rate, the year of birth	3.920	0.920	2.716	0.523
Birth cohort				
1960s	0.547	0.498		
1970s	0.453	0.498		
Age at first childbirth	29.547	3.070	25.678	3.382
First occupation				
Professional	0.155	0.362	0.101	0.301
Clerical	0.497	0.500	0.453	0.499
Service and sales	0.186	0.390	0.259	0.438
Manual labour	0.066	0.249	0.102	0.303
Self-employed	0.019	0.135	0.018	0.135
Teaching	0.077	0.266	0.067	0.250
Residence distance from parents, the year of birth				
Co-residence	0.199	0.399		
Proximate residence	0.176	0.381		
Parents lived further away than the same town, parents deceased	0.625	0.485		
Husband's annual income, the year of birth (10,000 yen)	477.257	220.797		
Husband's public sector employment, the year of birth	0.114	0.312		
Number of children at latest wave				
One			0.138	0.350
Two			0.550	0.498
More than three			0.313	0.464

Table S.3 Means and standard deviations of variables used in analyses of women's labour force re-entry after the first childbirth

N = 4819	Mean	S.D.
Reentry (Event occurred=1, not occurred=0)	0.084	0.277
Time		
The year of birth to 1 year since birth	0.175	0.380
2–3 years since birth	0.196	0.397
4–5 years since birth	0.177	0.382
6–9 years since birth	0.259	0.438
10–14 years since birth	0.144	0.351
15 years or over since birth	0.049	0.215
Educational attainment		
Junior high school or high school	0.435	0.496
Junior college	0.437	0.496
University	0.128	0.334
Unemployment rate	4.111	0.821
Birth cohort		
1960s	0.703	0.457
1970s	0.297	0.457
Age at first birth	27.456	3.350
First occupation		
Professional	0.095	0.293
Clerical	0.530	0.499
Service and sales	0.221	0.415
Manual labour	0.075	0.264
Self-employed	0.006	0.077
Teaching	0.073	0.260
Residence distance from parents		
Co-residence	0.247	0.431
Proximate residence	0.162	0.369
Parents lived further away than the same town, parents deceased	0.591	0.492
Husband's annual income (10,000 yen)	573.309	259.732
Husband's public sector employment	0.092	0.288
Number of children	1.828	0.756
Age of youngest child	3.508	3.541

Table S.4 Means and standard deviations of variables used in analyses of changes in employment status after re-entry as non-regular employee

N = 1450	Mean	S.D.
Change in employment status (Event occurred=1, not occurred=0)	0.208	0.578
Birth cohort		
1960s	0.781	0.414
1970s	0.219	0.414
Occupation at re-entry		
Professional	0.077	0.267
Clerical	0.235	0.424
Service and sales	0.414	0.493
Manual labour	0.230	0.421
Teaching	0.043	0.204
Husband's annual income (10,000 yen)	540.075	230.085
Age of youngest child	7.432	4.244

Table S.5 Means and standard deviations of variables used in analyses of women's labour force exit after the birth of the first child

N = 2099	Mean	S.D.
Exit (Event occurred=1, not occurred=0)	0.032	0.176
Time		
The year of birth to 1 year since birth	0.131	0.337
2–3 years since birth	0.133	0.340
4–5 years since birth	0.126	0.332
6–9 years since birth	0.232	0.422
10–14 years since birth	0.212	0.409
15 years or over since birth	0.167	0.373
Educational attainment		
Junior high school or high school	0.394	0.489
Junior college	0.428	0.495
University	0.178	0.382
Unemployment rate	4.167	0.782
Birth cohort		
1960s	0.755	0.430
1970s	0.245	0.430
Age at first childbirth	27.420	3.536
First occupation		
Professional	0.182	0.386
Clerical	0.363	0.481

Service and sales	0.154	0.361
Manual labour	0.096	0.294
Self-employed	0.038	0.192
Teaching	0.167	0.373
Residence distance from parents		
Co-residence	0.549	0.498
Proximate residence	0.175	0.380
Parents lived further away than the same town, parents deceased	0.276	0.447
Husband's annual income (10,000 yen)	499.496	268.727
Husband's public sector employment	0.248	0.432
Number of children	1.824	0.744
Age of youngest child	5.706	4.987

Table S.6 Means and standard deviations of variables used in analyses of single mothers' entry to regular employment

N = 406	Mean	S.D.
Change to regular employment (Event occurred = 1, not occurred = 0)	0.067	0.249
Time		
0 to 1 year since separation/divorce or death of spouse	0.394	0.489
2–4 years	0.345	0.476
5 years or over	0.261	0.440
Educational attainment		
Junior high school or high school	0.759	0.428
Junior college or university	0.241	0.428
Employment status at the year of separation/divorce or death of spouse		
Non-regular employee or self-employed	0.739	0.440
Not employed	0.261	0.440
Residence distance from parents		
Co-residence	0.300	0.459
Proximate residence	0.241	0.428
Parents lived further away than the same town, parents deceased	0.458	0.499
Unemployment rate	4.395	0.565
Age of youngest child	8.113	5.401

Table S.7 Means and standard deviations of variables used in analyses of single mothers' labour force exit

N = 520	Mean	S.D.
Exit (Event occurred=1, not occurred=0)	0.044	0.206
Time		
0 to 1 year since separation/divorce or death of spouse	0.381	0.486
2–4 years	0.358	0.480
5 years or over	0.262	0.440
Educational attainment		
Junior high school or high school	0.717	0.451
Junior college	0.229	0.420
University	0.054	0.226
Employment status at the year of separation/ divorce or death of spouse		
Regular employee	0.462	0.499
Non-regular employee or self-employed	0.538	0.499
Residence distance from parents		
Co-residence	0.308	0.462
Proximate residence	0.262	0.440
Parents lived further away than the same town, parents deceased	0.431	0.496
Unemployment rate	4.412	0.566
Age of youngest child	9.573	4.985
Remarriage (Event occurred = 1, not occurred = 0))	0.025	0.156

Index

Page numbers in bold indicate tables and figures.

For Product Safety Concerns and Information please contact our EU representative GPSR@taylorandfrancis.com Taylor & Francis Verlag GmbH, Kaufingerstraße 24, 80331 München, Germany

Batch number: 08153772

Printed by Printforce, the Netherlands